HAL•LEONARD GUITAR PLAY-ALONG

ACOUSTIC ANTHOLOGY

Tracking, mixing, and mastering by
Jake Johnson & Bill Maynard at Paradyme Productions
All guitars by Doug Boduch
Bass by Tom McGirr
Keyboards by Warren Wiegratz
Drums by Scott Schroedl

ISBN 978-1-4234-3068-1

For all works contained herein:
Unauthorized copying, arranging, adapting, recording or public
performance is an infringement of copyright.
Infringers are liable under the law.

Visit Hal Leonard Online at www.halleonard.com

HAL•LEONARD®
CORPORATION

7777 W. Bluemound Rd. P.O. Box 13819 Milwaukee, WI 53213

CONTENTS CD #1

CONTENTS CD #2

Dance with Me

Words and Music by John and Johanna Hall

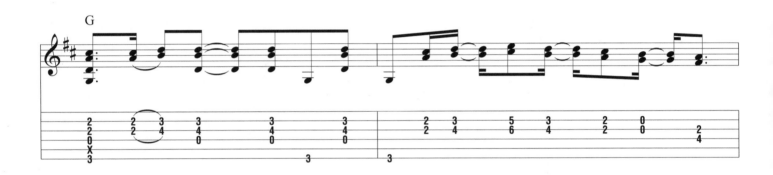

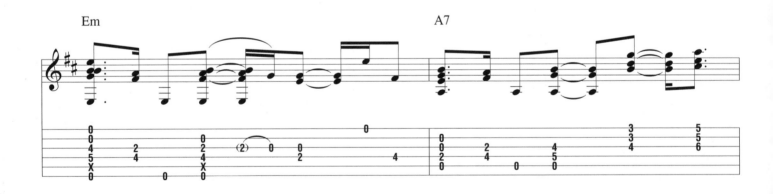

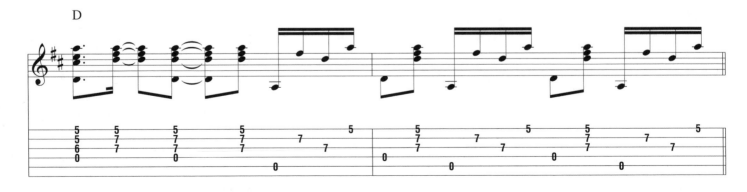

© 1975 (Renewed 2003) EMI BLACKWOOD MUSIC INC. and SIREN SONGS
All Rights Controlled and Administered by EMI BLACKWOOD MUSIC INC.
All Rights Reserved   International Copyright Secured   Used by Permission

Verse

1., 3., 4. Dance with __ me. __   I want __ to be __ your part - ner.
     2. *See additional lyrics*

Can't you __ see? __   The mus - ic is __ just start - ing.

Night is __ call - ing,   and I am __ fall - ing.

To Coda 1 ⊕
To Coda 2 ⊕

Dance with __ me. __

⊕ **Coda 1**

Harmonica/Mandolin Solo

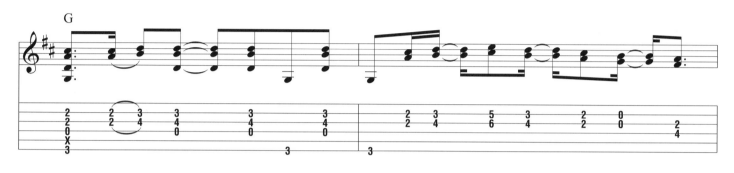

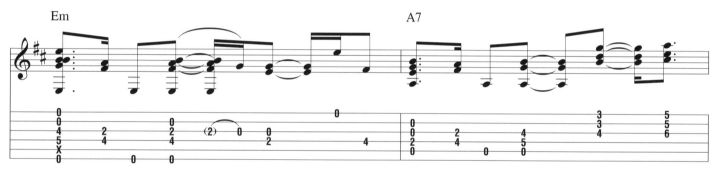

Bridge

Let it ____ lift you _____ off the ____ ground. ____

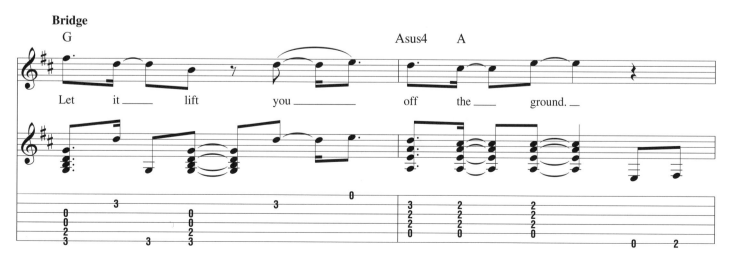

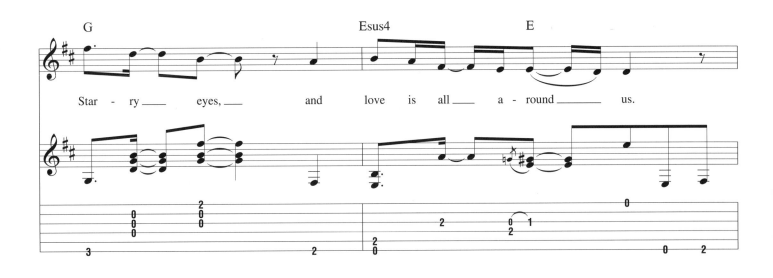

Star - ry eyes, and love is all a - round us.

I can take you where you want to go.

D.S. al Coda 2

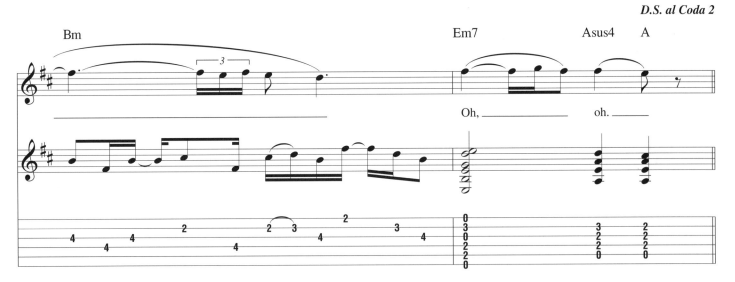

Oh, oh.

⊕ **Coda 2**

Outro

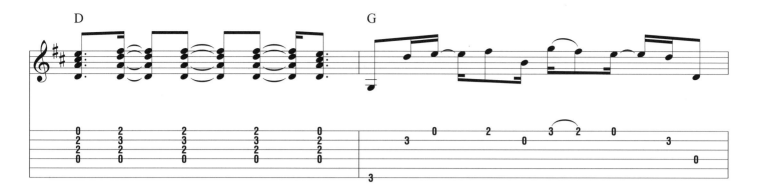

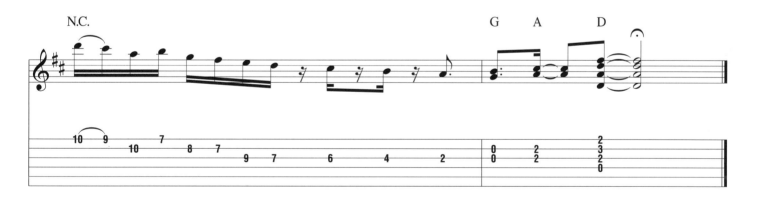

Additional Lyrics

2. Fantasy could never be so killing.
   I feel free.
   I hope that you are willing.
   Pick the beat up, and kick your feet up.
   Dance with me.

Don't Ask Me Why

Words and Music by Billy Joel

Capo III

Intro
Moderately ♩ = 98

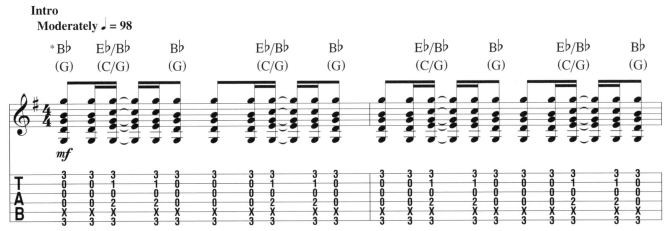

* Symbols in parentheses represent chord names respective to capoed guitar. Symbols above reflect actual sounding chords.
Capoed fret is "0" in tab.

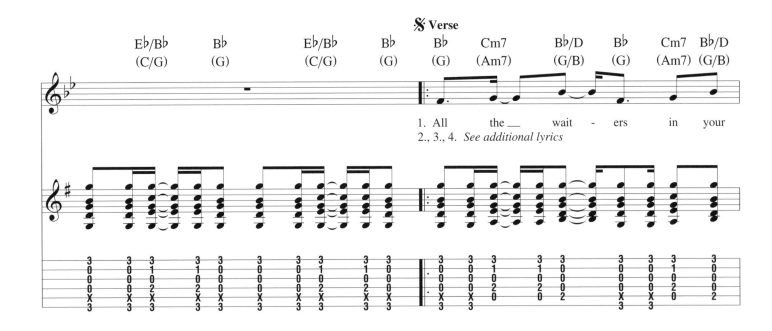

1. All the ___ wait - ers in your
2., 3., 4. *See additional lyrics*

grand ca - fe ___ leave their ___ ta - bles when you

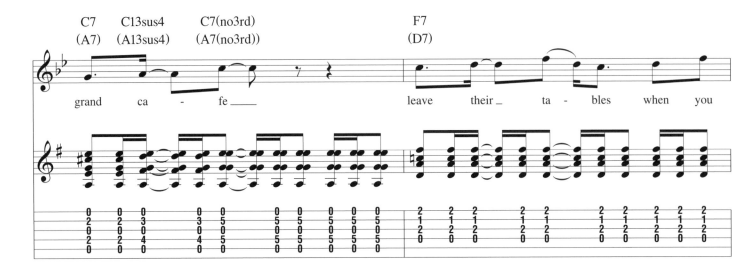

© 1980 IMPULSIVE MUSIC
All Rights Reserved   International Copyright Secured   Used by Permission

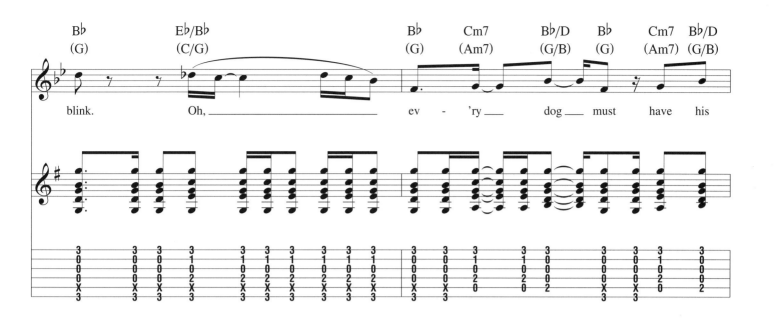

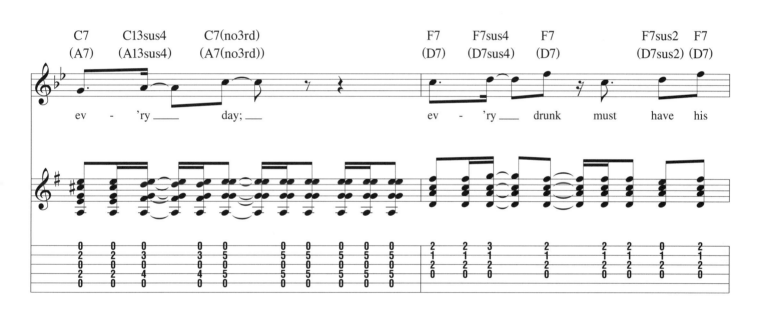

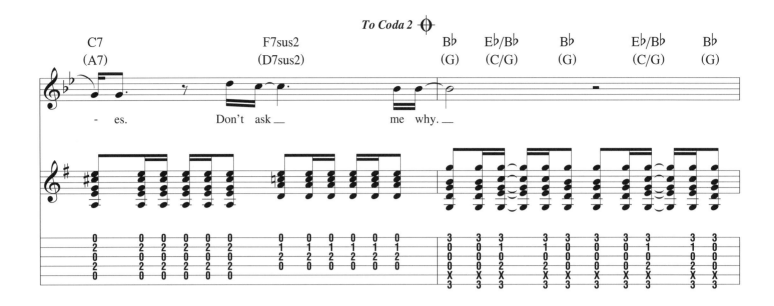

To Coda 2 ⊕

C7 (A7) F7sus2 (D7sus2) Bb (G) Eb/Bb (C/G) Bb (G) Eb/Bb (C/G) Bb (G)

- es.   Don't ask __ me why. __

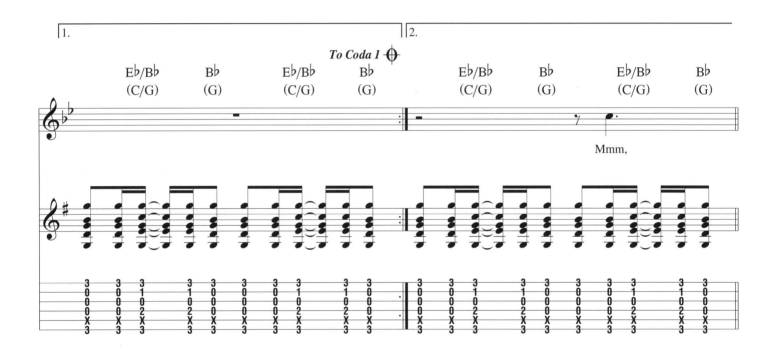

1.

To Coda 1 ⊕

Eb/Bb (C/G) Bb (G) Eb/Bb (C/G) Bb (G)

2.

Eb/Bb (C/G) Bb (G) Eb/Bb (C/G) Bb (G)

Mmm,

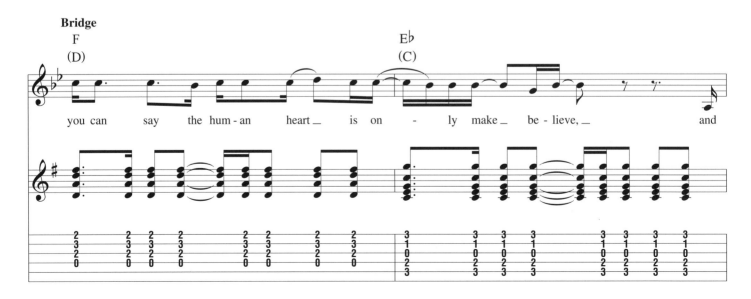

Bridge

F (D) Eb (C)

you can say the hum-an heart __ is on - ly make __ be - lieve, __ and

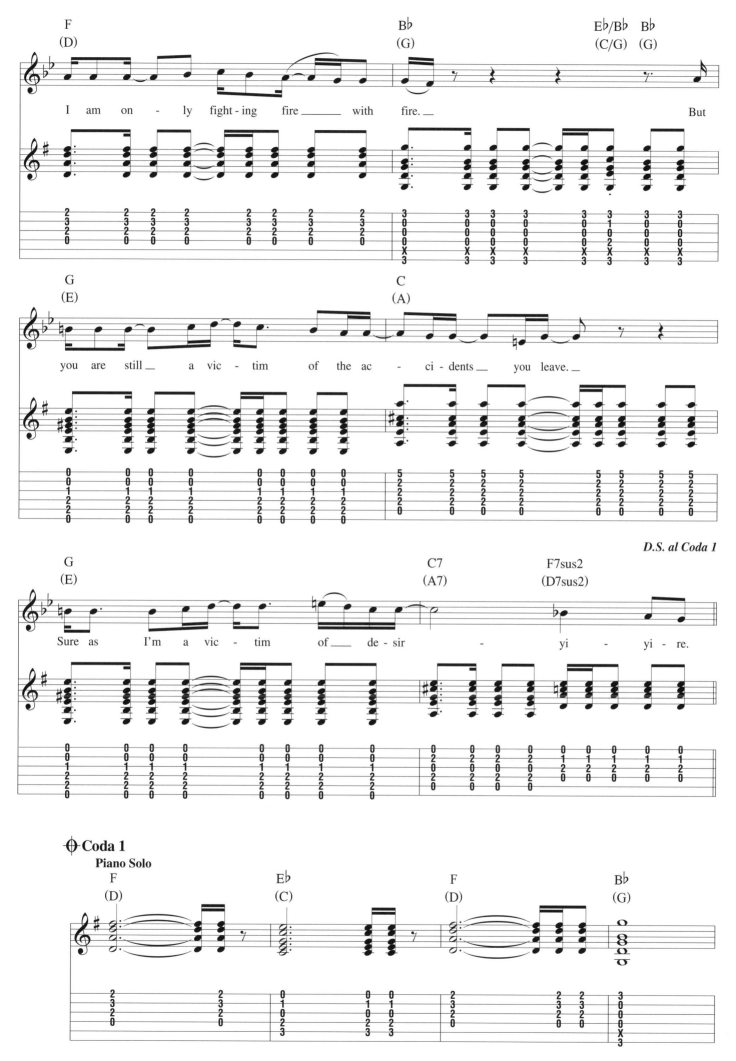

D.S. al Coda 1

Coda 1

Piano Solo

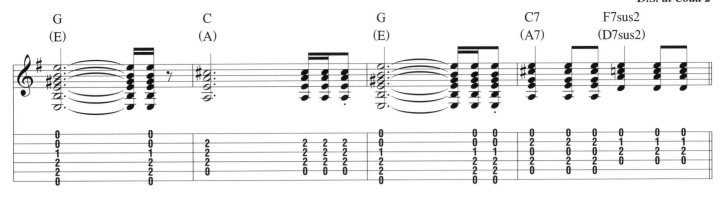

Coda 2

Outro

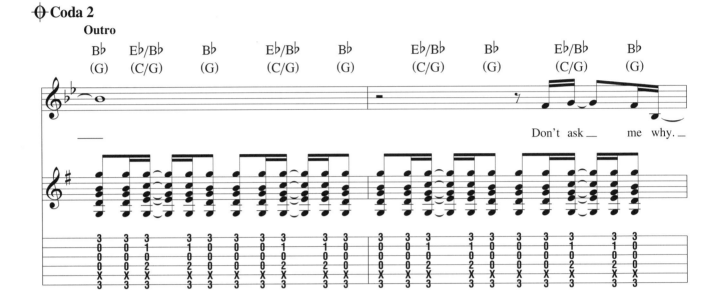

Don't ask __ me why. __

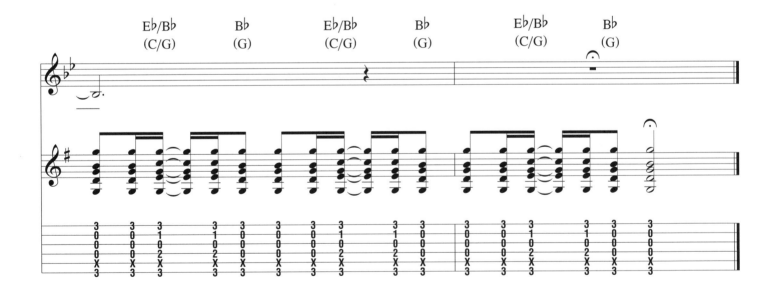

Additional Lyrics

2. All your life you had to stand in line,
   Still you're standing on your feet.
   Oh, all your choices made you change your mind,
   Now your calendar's complete.
   Don't wait for answers;
   Just take your chances.
   Don't ask me why.

3. All the servants in your new hotel
   Throw their roses at your feet.
   Oh, fool them all but, baby, I can tell
   You're no stranger to the street.
   Don't ask for favors;
   Don't talk to strangers.
   Don't ask me why.

4. Yesterday you were an only child,
   Now your ghosts have gone away.
   Oh, you can kill them in the classic style.
   Now you "parlezvous Français."
   Don't look for answers;
   You took your chances.
   Don't ask me why.

Fooling Yourself
(The Angry Young Man)

Words and Music by Tommy Shaw

Drop D tuning:
(low to high) D-A-D-G-B-E

*Chord symbols reflect implied harmony.

Copyright © 1977 ALMO MUSIC CORP. and STYGIAN SONGS
Copyright Renewed
All Rights Controlled and Administered by ALMO MUSIC CORP.
All Rights Reserved   Used by Permission

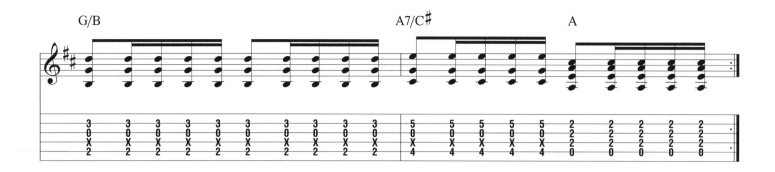

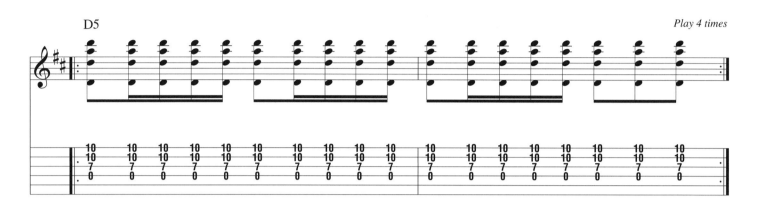

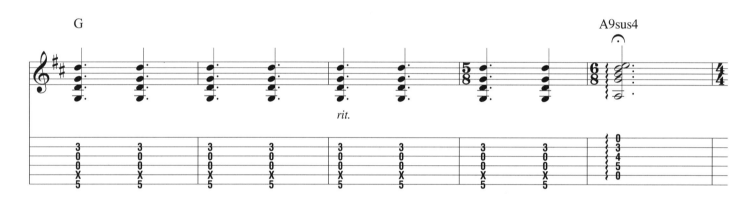

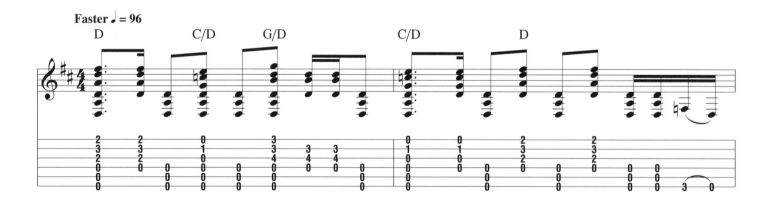

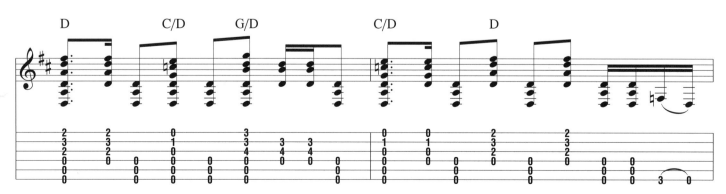

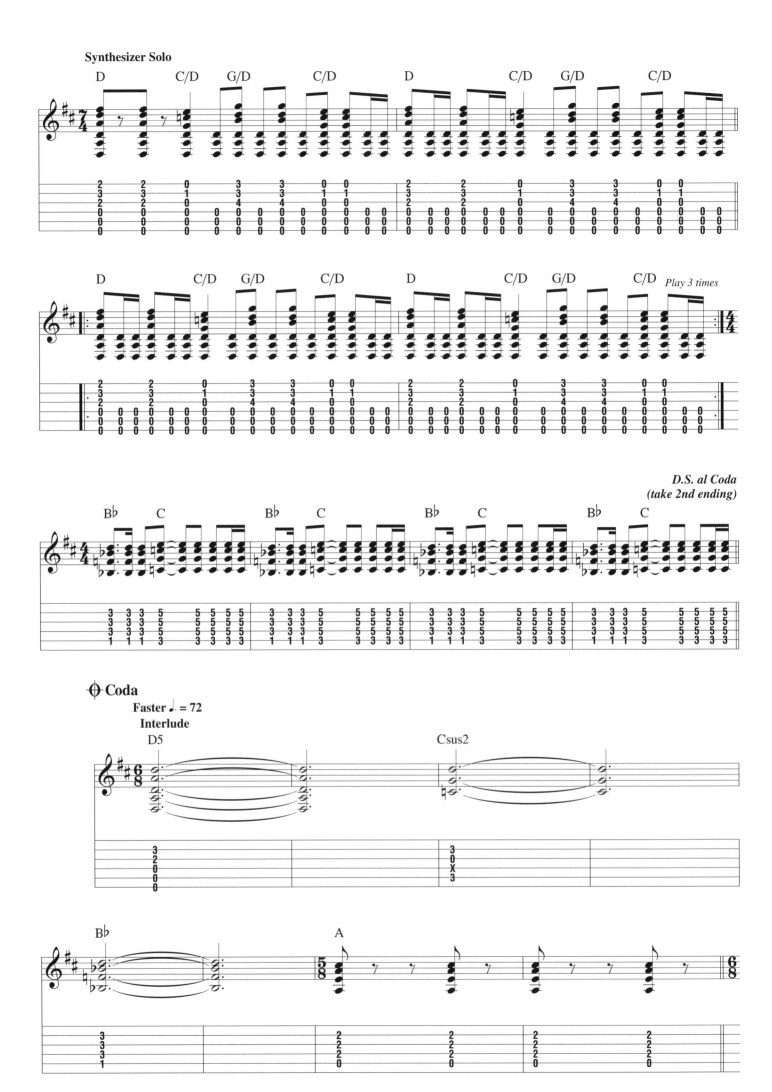

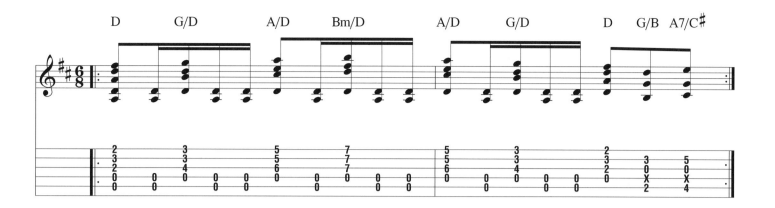

Outro-Synth. Solo

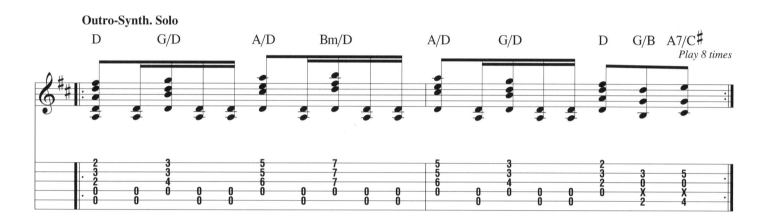

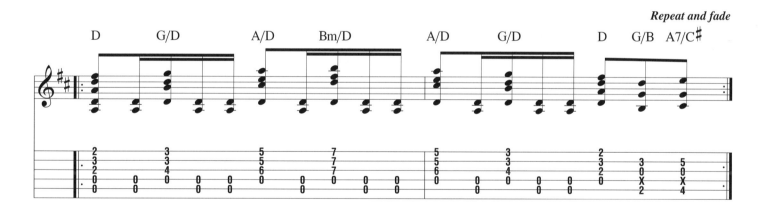

Additional Lyrics

2. Why must you be such an angry young man
   When your future looks quite bright to me?
   And how can there be such a sinister plan
   That could hide such a lamb,
   Such a caring young man?

Give a Little Bit

Words and Music by Rick Davies and Roger Hodgson

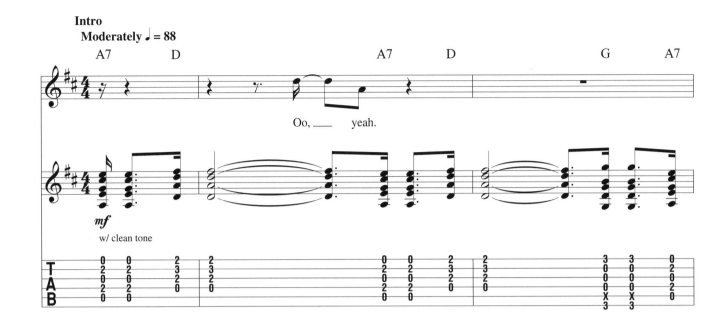

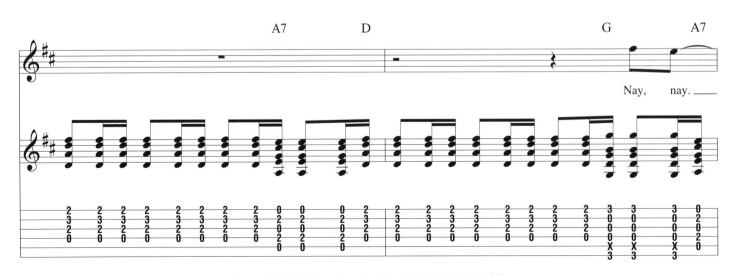

Copyright © 1977 ALMO MUSIC CORP. and DELICATE MUSIC
Copyright Renewed
All Rights Controlled and Administered by ALMO MUSIC CORP.
All Rights Reserved Used by Permission

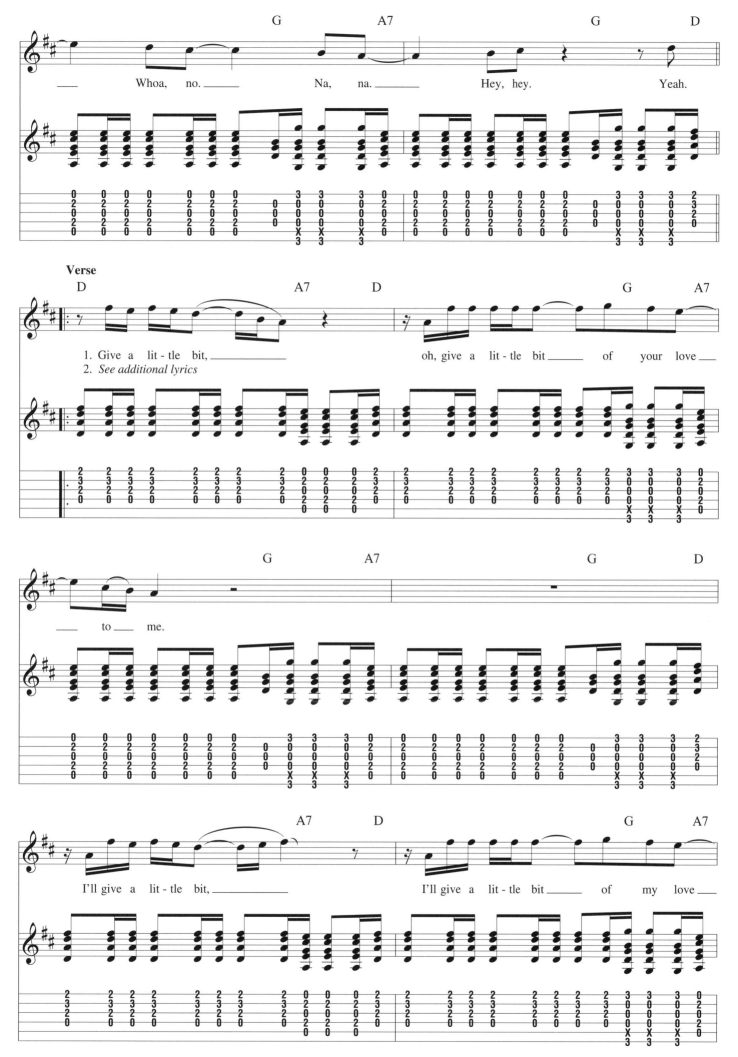

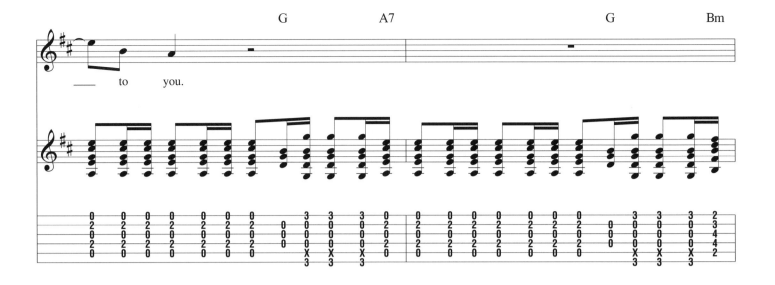

to you.

There's so much ___ that we need ___ to share, ___ so

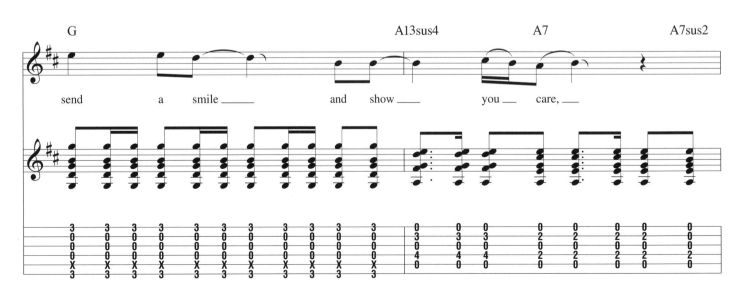

send a smile ___ and show ___ you ___ care, ___

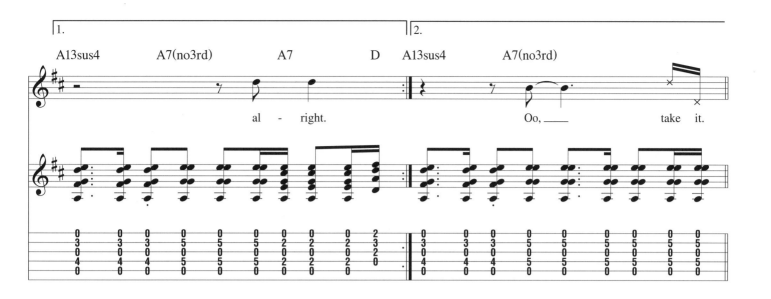

Interlude

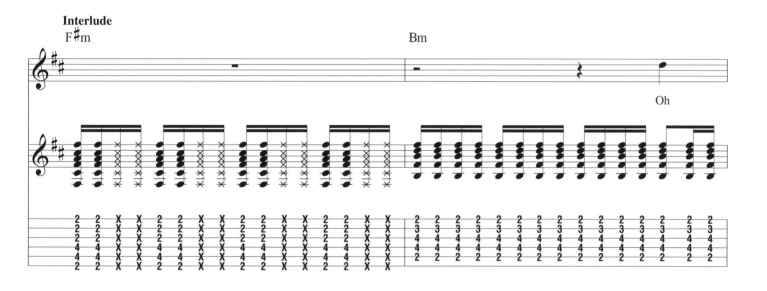

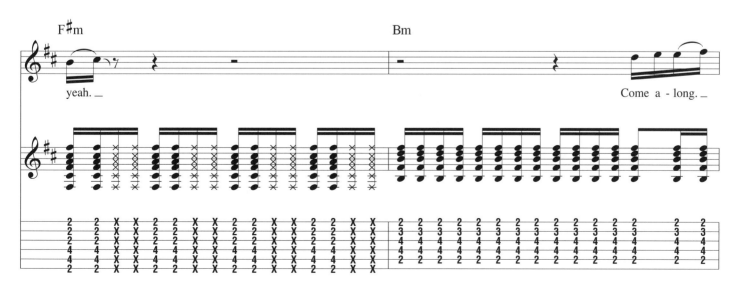

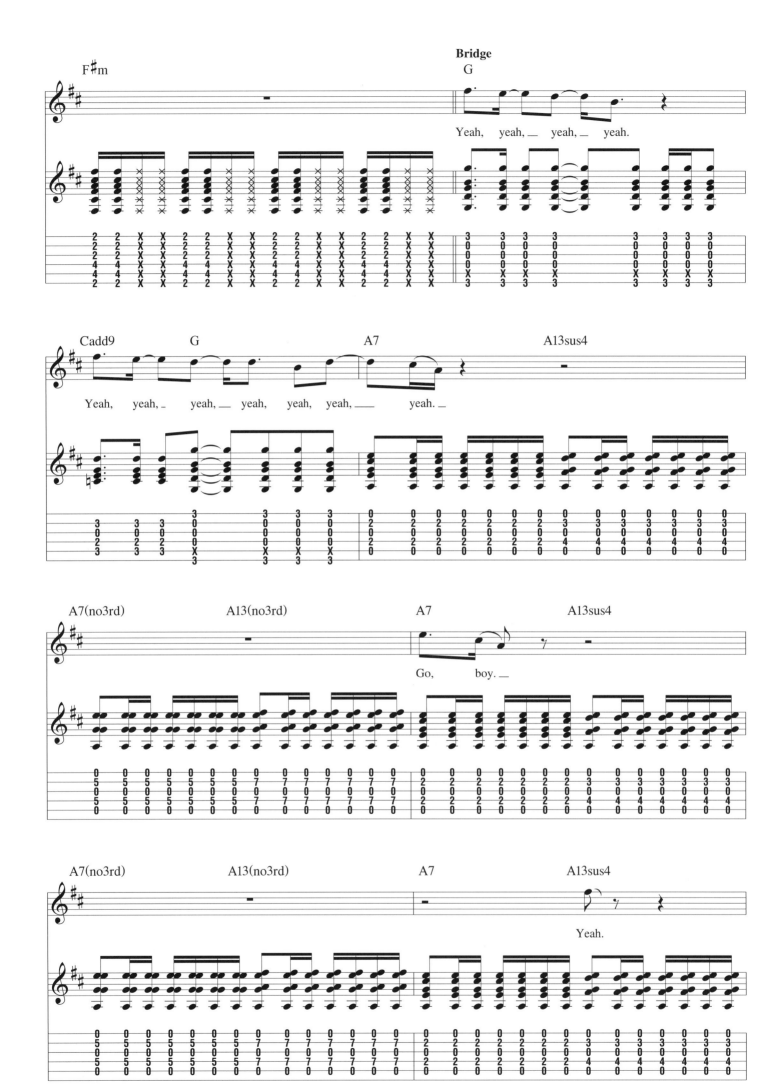

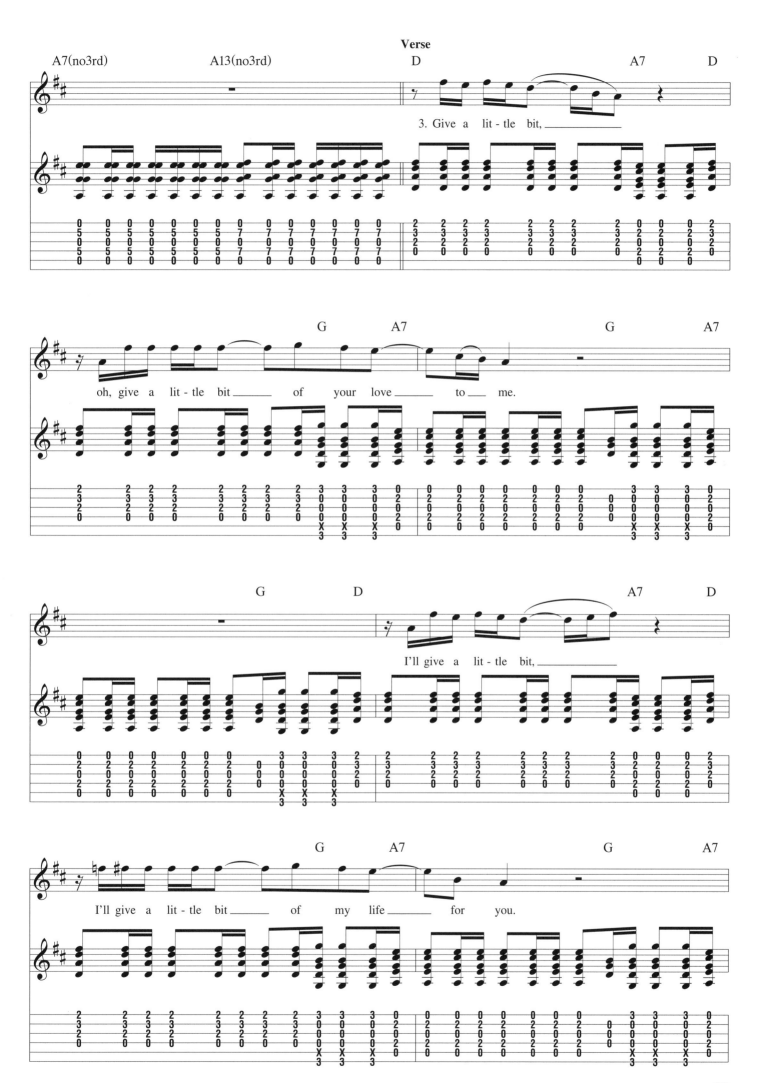

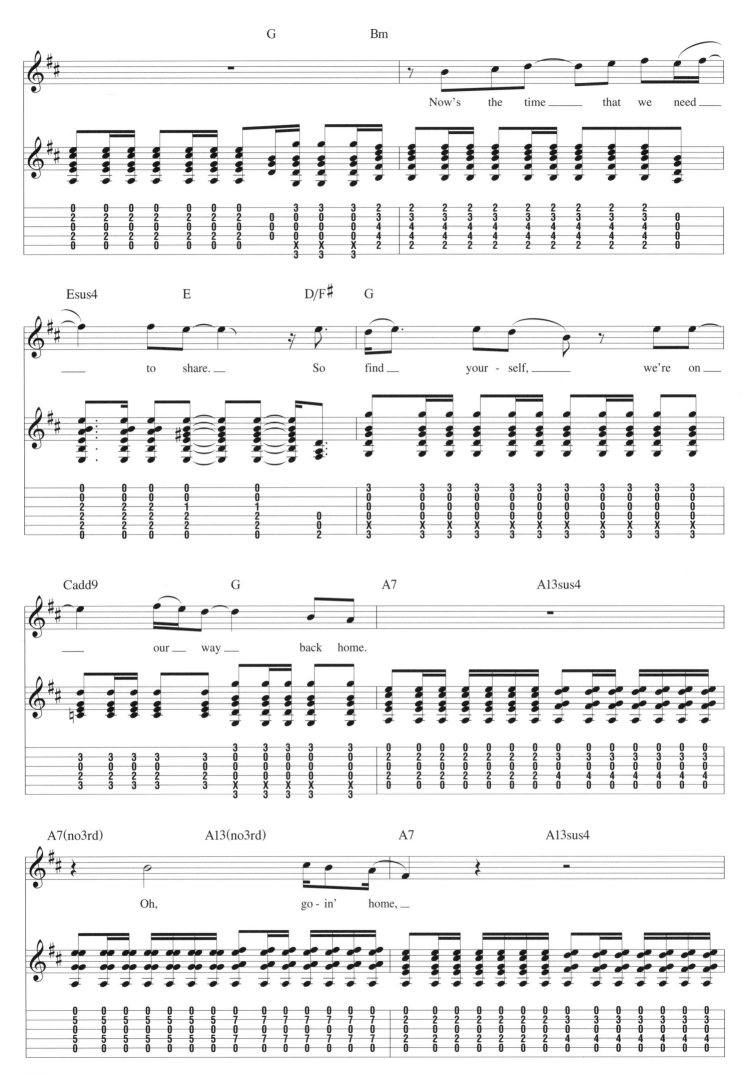

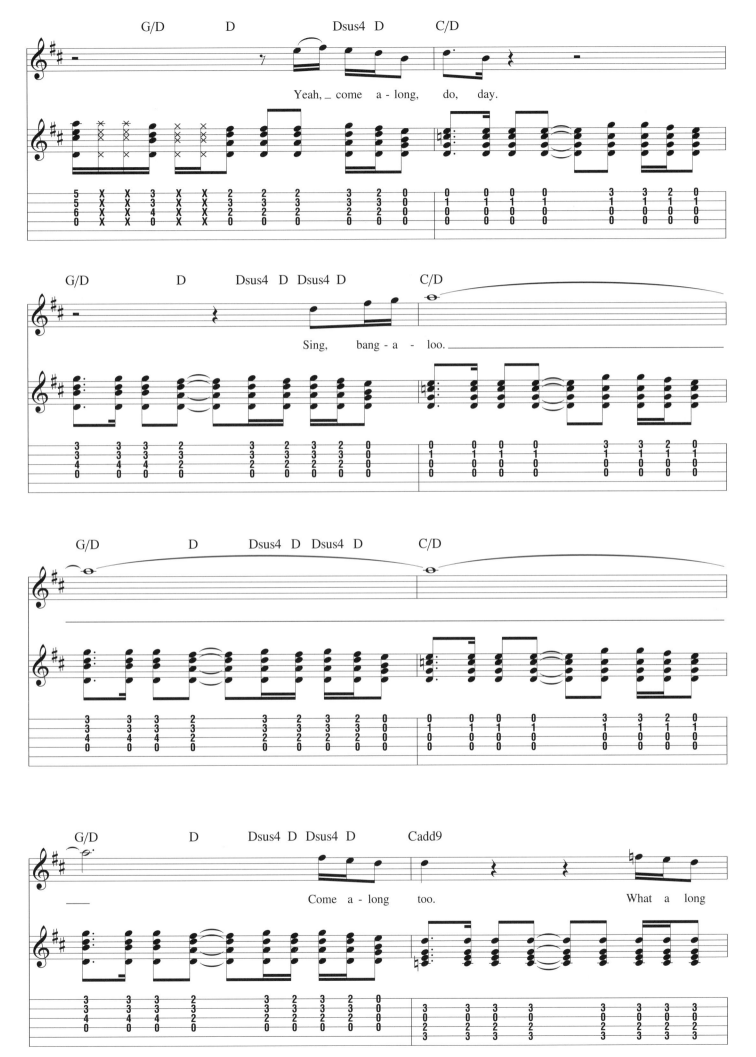

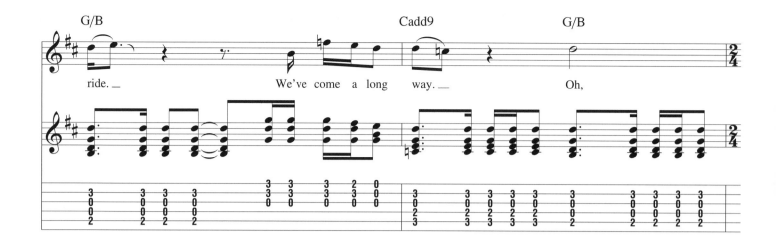

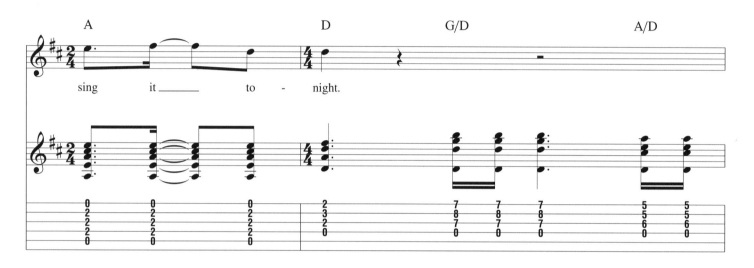

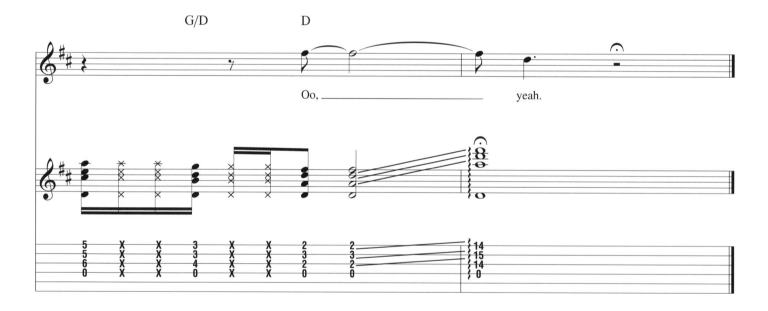

Additional Lyrics

2. I'll give a little bit,
I'll give a little bit of my life for you.
So give a little bit,
Oh, give a little bit of your time to me.
See the man with the lonely eyes.
Oh, take his hand, you'll be surprised.
Oo, take it.

Jack and Diane

Words and Music by John Mellencamp

© 1982 EMI FULL KEEL MUSIC
All Rights Reserved International Copyright Secured Used by Permission

Interlude

Verse

2. Suck-in' on a chil-i dog out-side the Tast-ee Freez; ____

3. *See additional lyrics*

Di-ane ____ sit-tin' on Jack-ie's lap, ____ he's got his hands be-tween ____ her knees.____

CONTENTS CD #2

Dance with Me

Words and Music by John and Johanna Hall

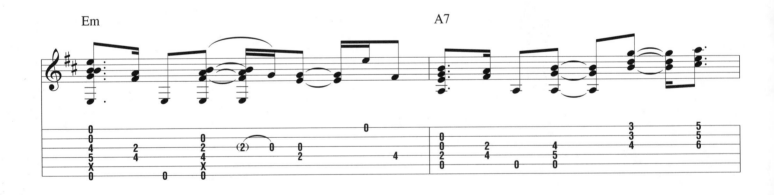

© 1975 (Renewed 2003) EMI BLACKWOOD MUSIC INC. and SIREN SONGS
All Rights Controlled and Administered by EMI BLACKWOOD MUSIC INC.
All Rights Reserved   International Copyright Secured   Used by Permission

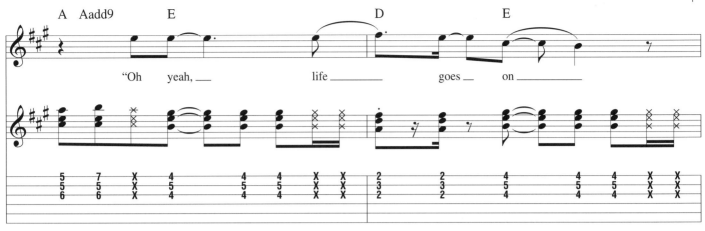

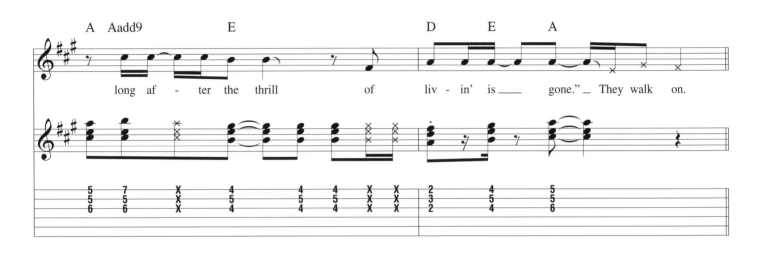

2nd time, D.S. al Coda

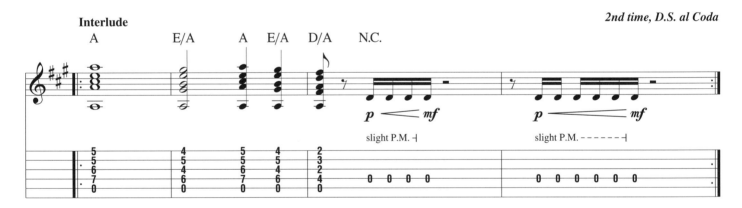

 Coda

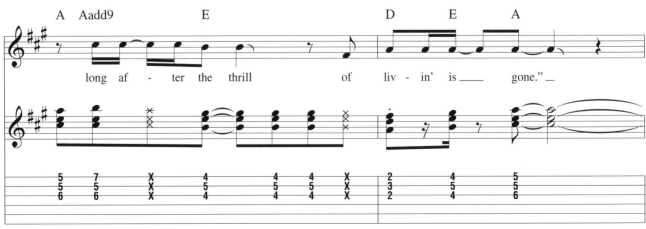

Chorus

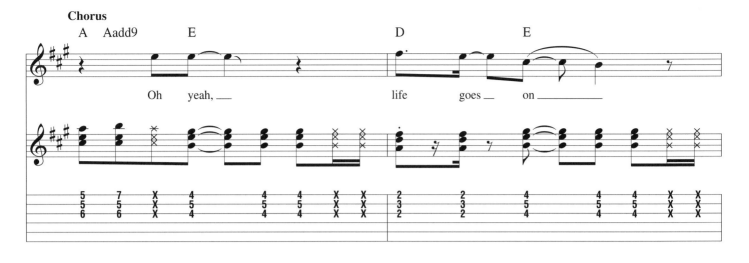

Oh yeah, ___ life goes ___ on ___

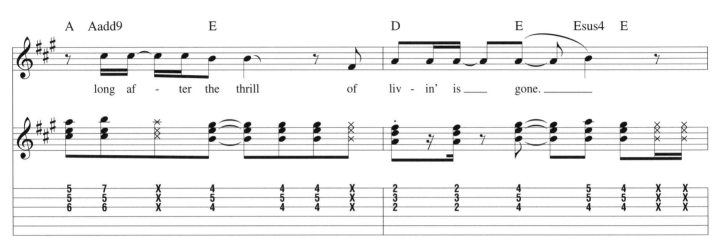

long af - ter the thrill of liv - in' is ___ gone. ___

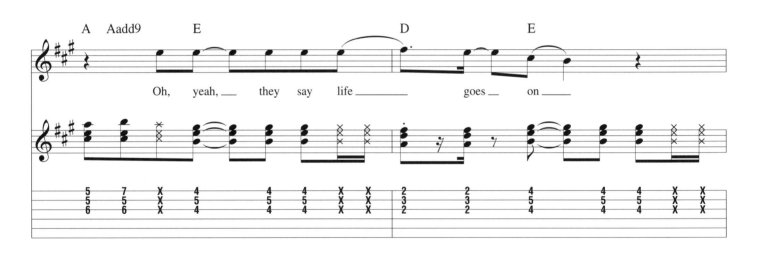

Oh, yeah, ___ they say life ___ goes ___ on ___

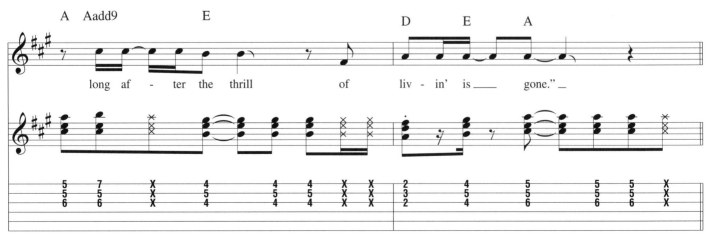

long af - ter the thrill of liv - in' is ___ gone." _

Outro-Verse

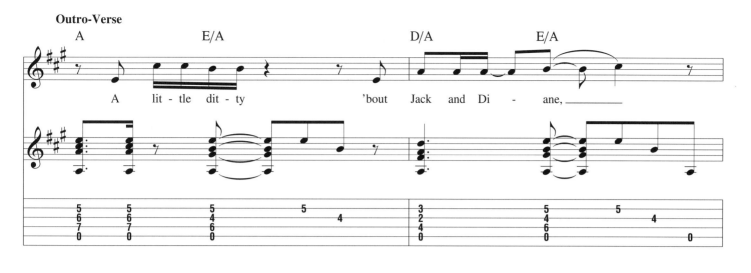

A little ditty 'bout Jack and Di - ane, _____

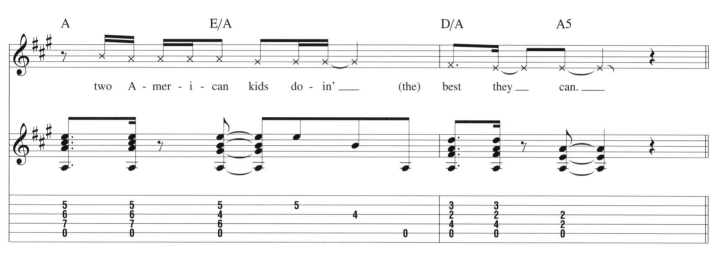

two A - mer - i - can kids do - in' ___ (the) best they __ can. __

Play 4 times & fade

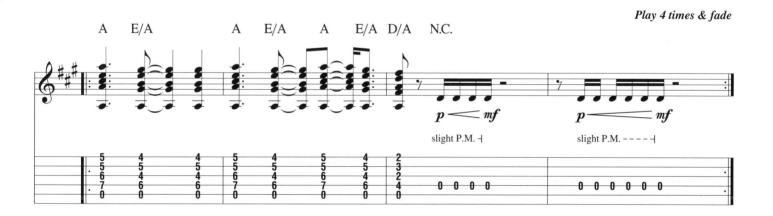

slight P.M. ⌐   slight P.M. - - - - ⌐

Additional Lyrics

3. Jackie sits back, collects his thoughts for the moment.
Scratches his head and does his best James Dean.
"Well, then there Diane, we oughta run off to the city."
Diane says, "Baby, you ain't missin' nothing." But Jackie say, ah,

Chorus 2. "Oh yeah, life goes on
Long after the thrill of livin' is gone."
"Oh yeah," they say, "life goes on
Long after the thrill of livin' is gone."

I'll Have to Say I Love You in a Song

Words and Music by Jim Croce

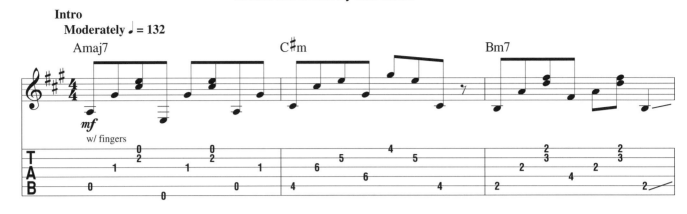

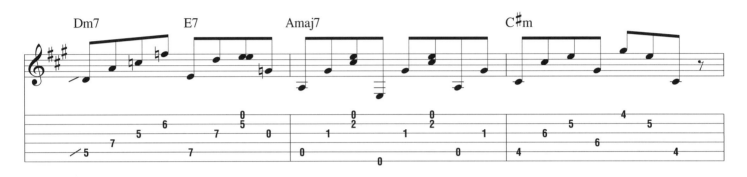

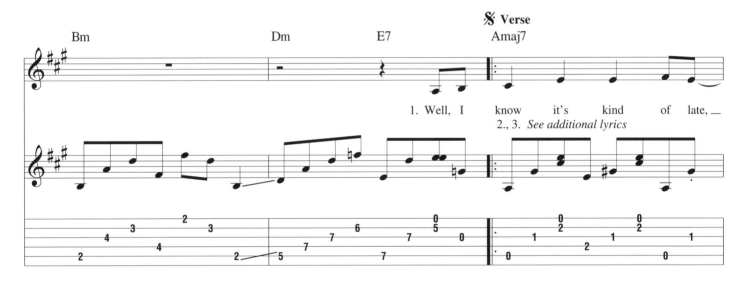

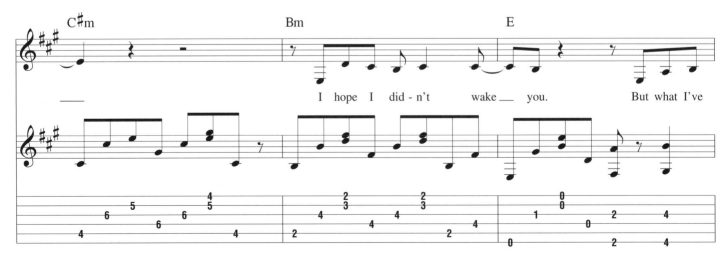

© 1973 (Renewed 2001) TIME IN A BOTTLE PUBLISHING and CROCE PUBLISHING
All Rights Controlled and Administered by EMI APRIL MUSIC INC.
All Rights Reserved   International Copyright Secured   Used by Permission

have to say ___ I love ___ you in a song. ___

3. Yeah, I

Coda

Outro

Additional Lyrics

2. Yeah, I know it's kind of strange,
   But ev'ry time I'm near you
   I just run out of things to say.
   I know you'd understand.

3. Yeah, I know it's kind of late,
   I hope I didn't wake you.
   But there's something that I just gotta say.
   I know you'd understand.

The Joker

Words and Music by Steve Miller, Eddie Curtis and Ahmet Ertegun

Tune down one step:
(low to high) D-G-C-F-A-D

Verse
Moderately slow ♩ = 82

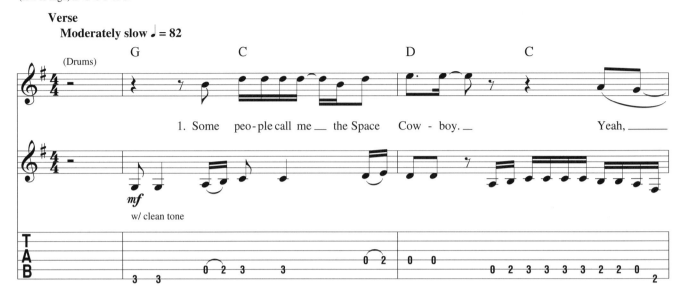

1. Some peo-ple call me ___ the Space Cow-boy. ___ Yeah, ___

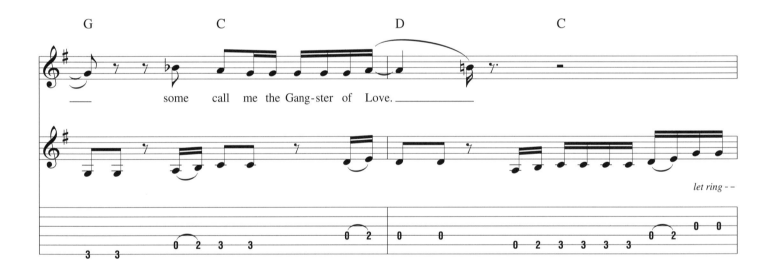

___ some call me the Gang-ster of Love. ___

Some peo-ple call me Maur - ice, 'cause I

Copyright © 1973 by Sailor Music and Warner-Tamerlane Publishing Corp.
Copyright Renewed
All Rights Reserved Used by Permission

Chorus

*let ring

*Next 16 meas.

Verse

You're the cut - est thing _ that I ev - er did see. _____ I

real - ly love _ your peach - es, want to shake your tree. _____

Love - y dove - y, love-y dove-y, love - y dove-y all the time. _____

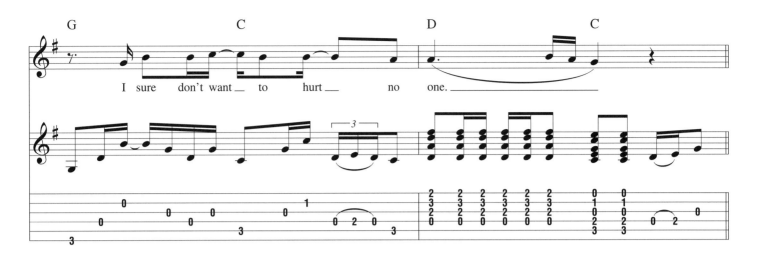

I sure don't want to hurt no one.

Guitar Solo

w/ reverb & wah-wah

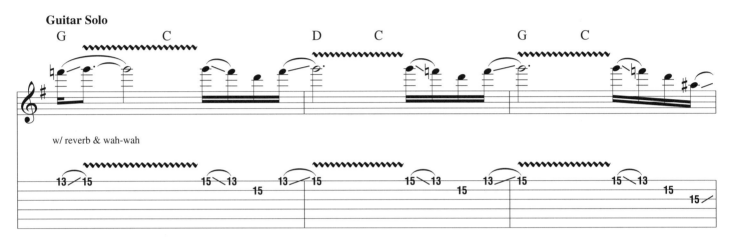

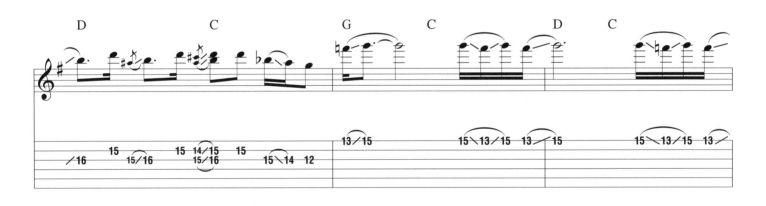

Woo - hoo. _____ Woo - hoo. _____

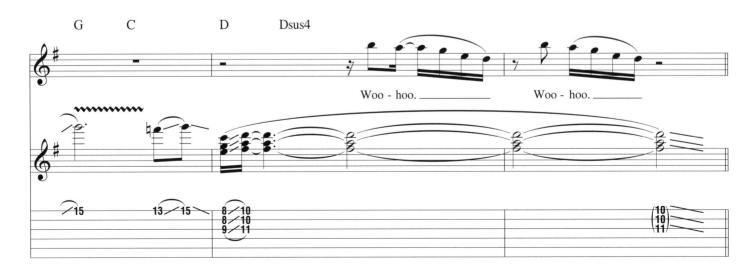

Outro-Verse

Leader of the Band

Words and Music by Dan Fogelberg

* Chord symbols in parentheses represent chord names respective to capoed guitar.
Symbols above reflect actual sounding chords. Capoed fret is "0" in tab.

1. An on-ly child_ a-lone_
2., 3., 4. *See additional lyrics*

**4th time, play bottom note of beat 1 only.

© 1981 EMI APRIL MUSIC INC. and HICKORY GROVE MUSIC
All Rights Controlled and Administered by EMI APRIL MUSIC INC.
All Rights Reserved International Copyright Secured Used by Permission

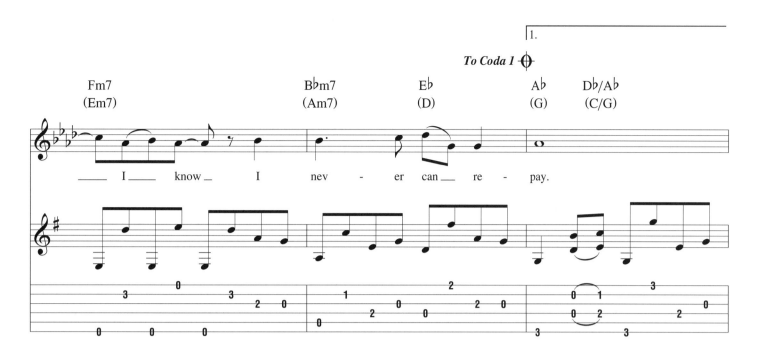

I know I nev-er can re-pay.

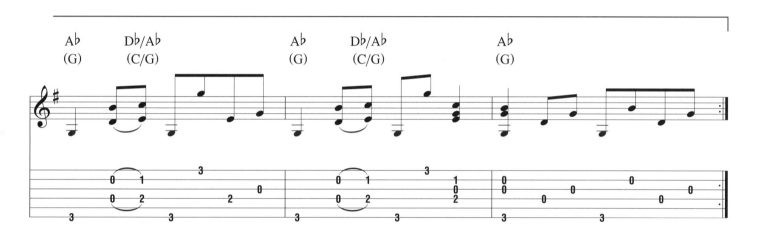

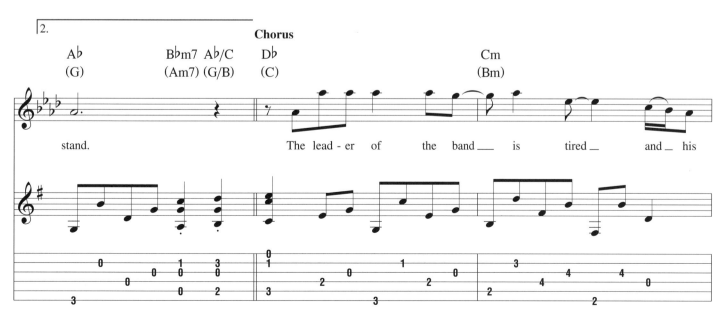

stand. The lead-er of the band is tired and his

D.S. al Coda 2
(take 2nd ending)

Coda 2

band. I am the liv - ing___ leg - a - cy to the

lead - er of _____ the band. _____

Additional Lyrics

2. A quiet man of music,
   Denied a simpler fate.
   He tried to be a soldier once
   But his music wouldn't wait.
   He earned his love through discipline,
   A thund'ring velvet hand.
   His gentle means of sculpting souls
   Took me years to understand.

3. My brothers' lives were diff'rent,
   For they heard another call.
   One went to Chicago,
   And the other to St. Paul.
   And I'm in Colorado,
   When I'm not in some hotel,
   Living out this life I've chose
   And gone to know so well.

4. I thank you for the music
   And your stories of the road.
   I thank you for the freedom
   When it came my time to go.
   I thank you for the kindness
   And the times when you got tough.
   And Papa, I don't think I said,
   "I love you" near enough.

Love Will Keep Us Alive

Words and Music by Peter Vale, Jim Capaldi and Paul Carrack

© 1994 EMI VIRGIN MUSIC LTD., FREEDOM SONGS LTD. and PLANGENT VISIONS MUSIC LTD.
All Rights for EMI VIRGIN MUSIC LTD. Controlled and Administered by EMI VIRGIN SONGS, INC.
All Rights for FREEDOM SONGS LTD. Controlled and Administered by MUSIC OF WINDSWEPT
All Rights Reserved   International Copyright Secured   Used by Permission

Additional Lyrics

2. Don't you worry,
   Sometimes you've just got to let it ride.
   The world is changing right before your eyes.
   Now I've found you,
   There's no more emptiness inside.
   When we're hungry,
   Love will keep us alive.

Midnight Rider

Words and Music by Gregg Allman and Robert Kim Payne

Copyright © 1970 by Unichappell Music Inc. and Elijah Blue Music
Copyright Renewed
International Copyright Secured   All Rights Reserved

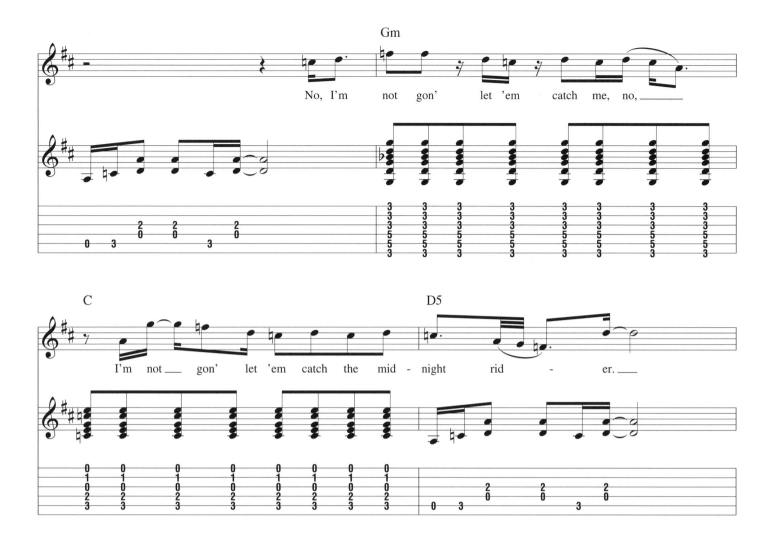

Additional Lyrics

2. And I don't own the clothes I'm wearin'.
   And the road goes on forever.
   And I've got one more silver dollar.
   But I'm not gon' let 'em catch me, no,
   Not gon' let 'em catch the midnight rider.

3. And I've gone past the point of carin'.
   Some ol' bed I'll soon be sharin'.
   And I've dropped one more silver dollar.
   But I'm not gon' let 'em catch me, no,
   Not gon' let 'em catch the midnight rider.

More Than a Feeling

Words and Music by Tom Scholz

Copyright © 1976 Pure Songs
Copyright Renewed
All Rights Administered by Next Decade Entertainment, Inc.
All Rights Reserved Used by Permission

Chorus

more than a feel - ing _____ when I

see that old song _____ they used to play. _____ And

I be - gin dream - ing _____ till I

see Mar - i - anne _____ walk a - way. _____ I see my Mar -

She slipped a - way,

ah,   ah.

Outro-Chorus

It's more than a feel - ing _____ when I hear that old song _____ they used to play. _____ And I be - gin dream - ing _____ till I see Mar - i - anne _____ walk a -

Additional Lyrics

2. So many people have come and gone,
    Their faces fade as the years go by.
    Yet I still recall as I wander on,
    As clear as the sun in the summer sky.

Rocky Raccoon

Words and Music by John Lennon and Paul McCartney

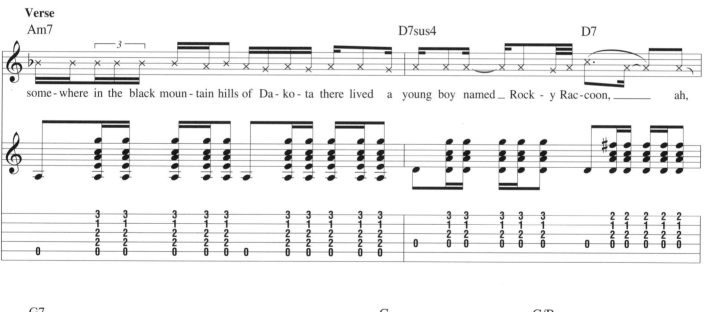

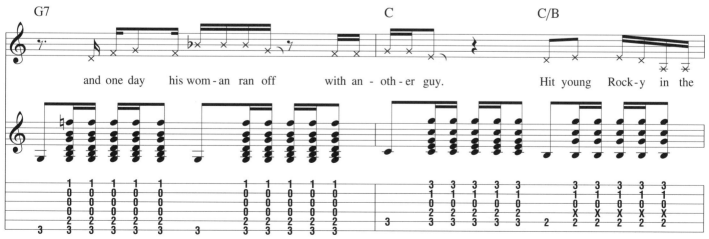

Copyright © 1968, 1969 Sony/ATV Music Publishing LLC
Copyright Renewed
All Rights Administered by Sony/ATV Music Publishing LLC, 8 Music Square West, Nashville, TN 37203
International Copyright Secured   All Rights Reserved

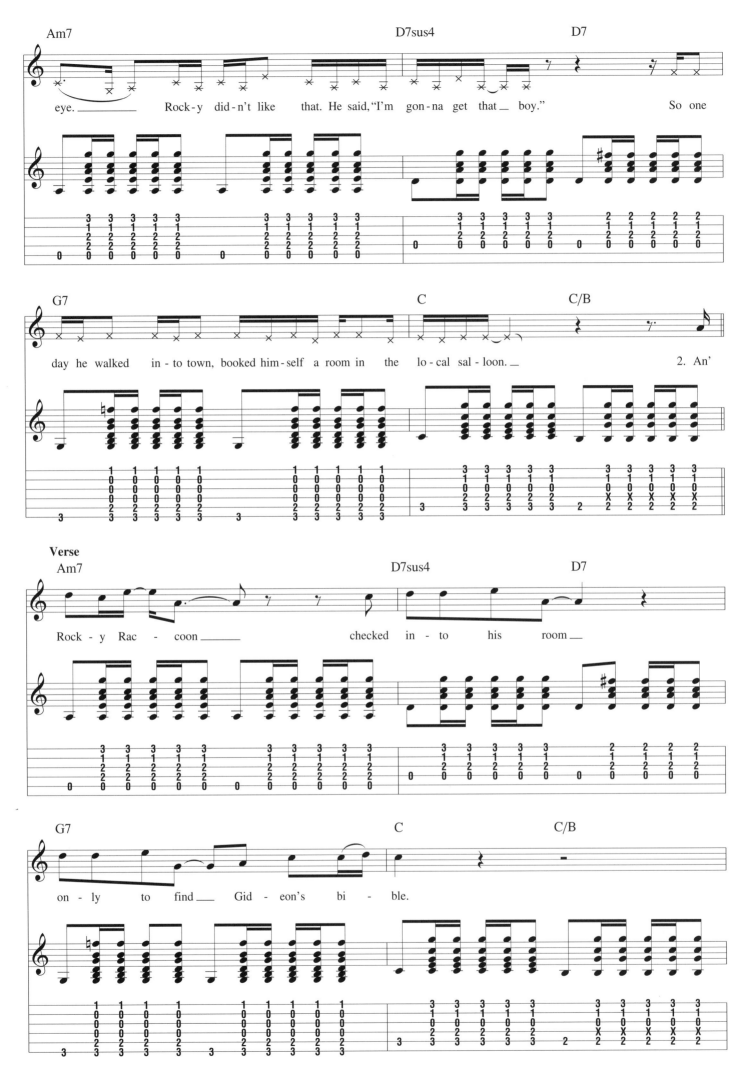

Piano Solo

Teach Your Children

Words and Music by Graham Nash

Drop D tuning:
(low to high) D-A-D-G-B-E

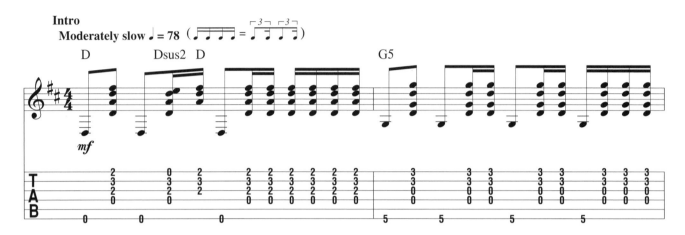

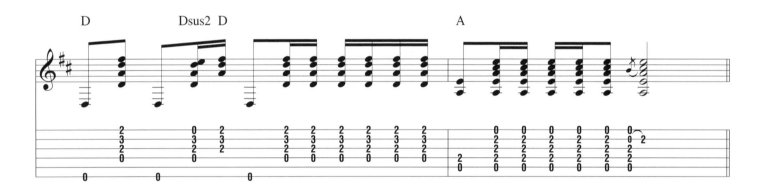

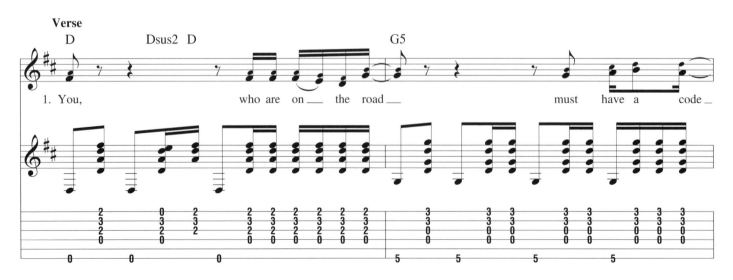

Copyright © 1970 Nash Notes
Copyright Renewed
All Rights Administered by Sony/ATV Music Publishing LLC, 8 Music Square West, Nashville, TN 37203
International Copyright Secured   All Rights Reserved

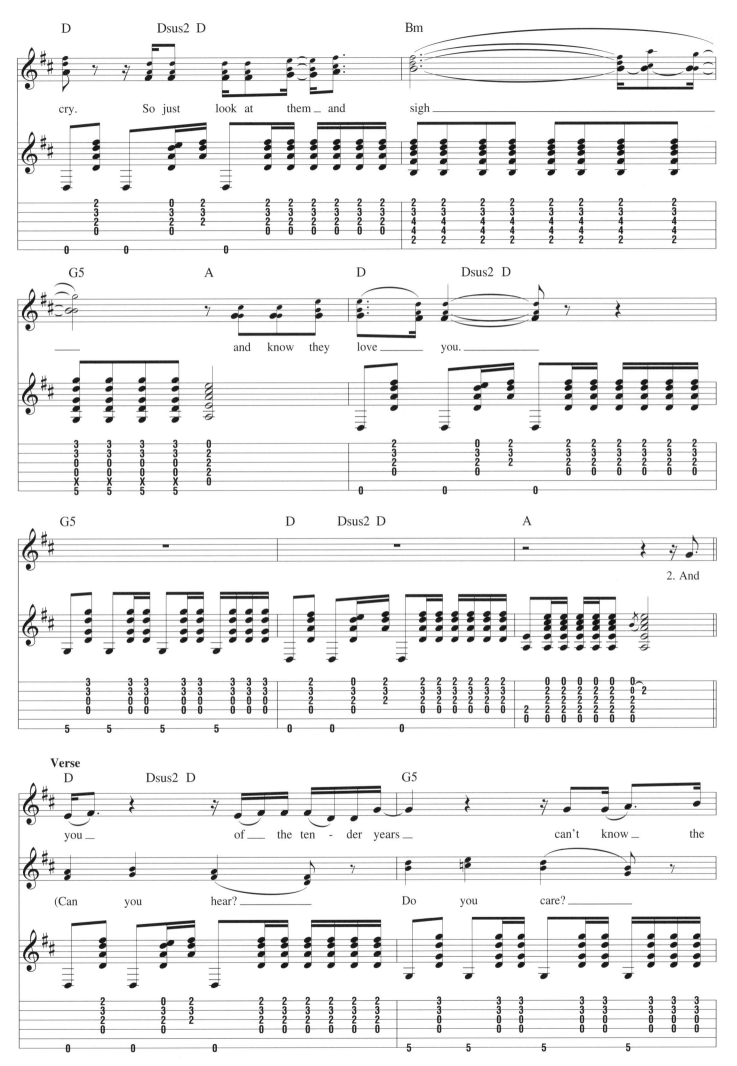

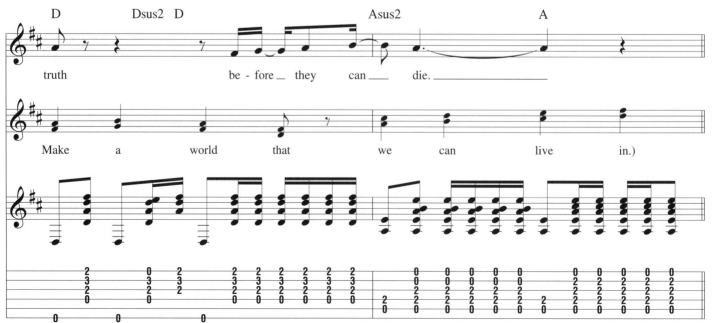

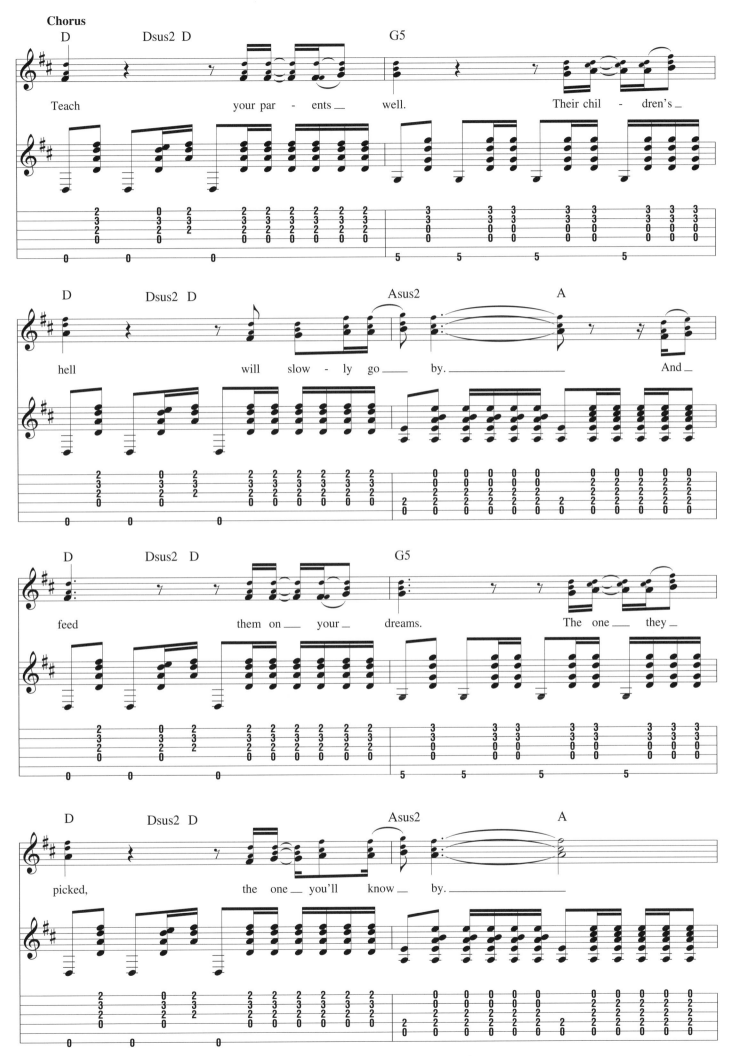

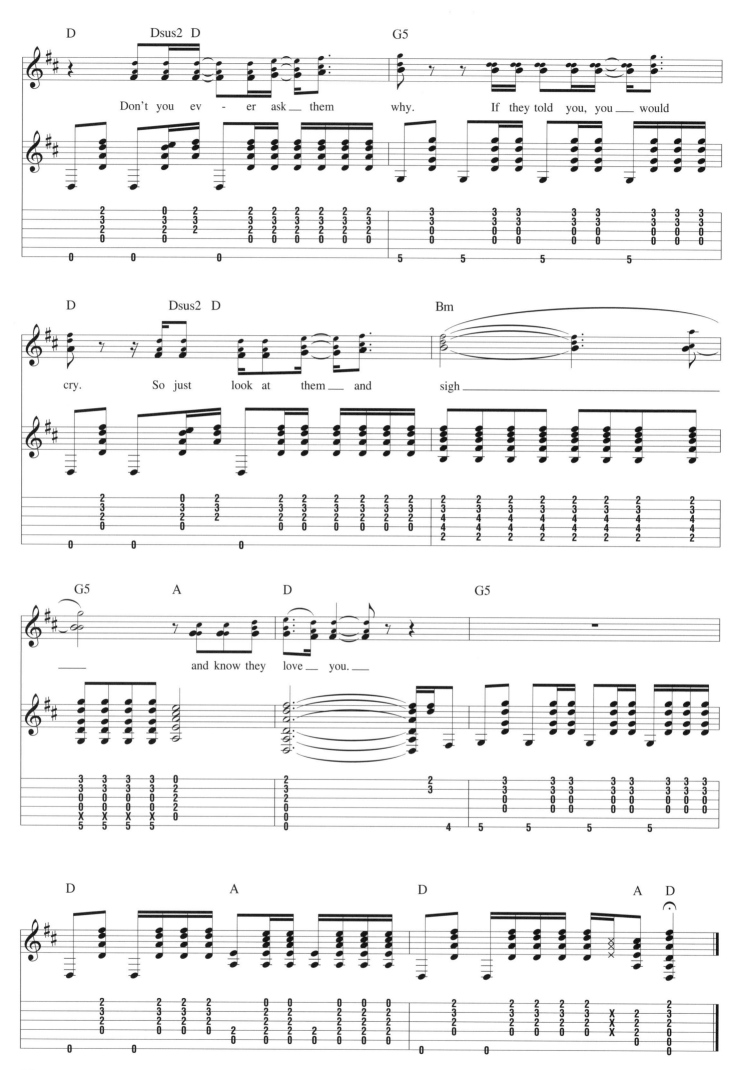

Time for Me to Fly

Words and Music by Kevin Cronin

Drop D tuning:
(low to high) D-A-D-G-B-E

Intro
Moderately ♩ = 82

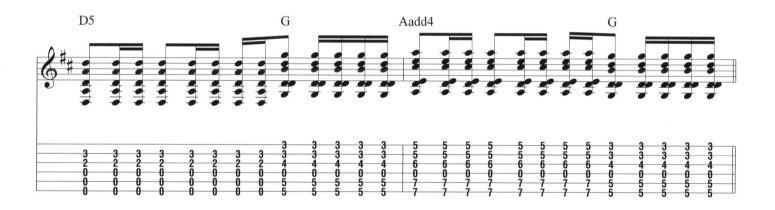

Verse

1. I've been a-round ___ for ___ you, I've been up and down ___ for ___ you, but I

Copyright © 1978 Fate Music (ASCAP)
International Copyright Secured All Rights Reserved

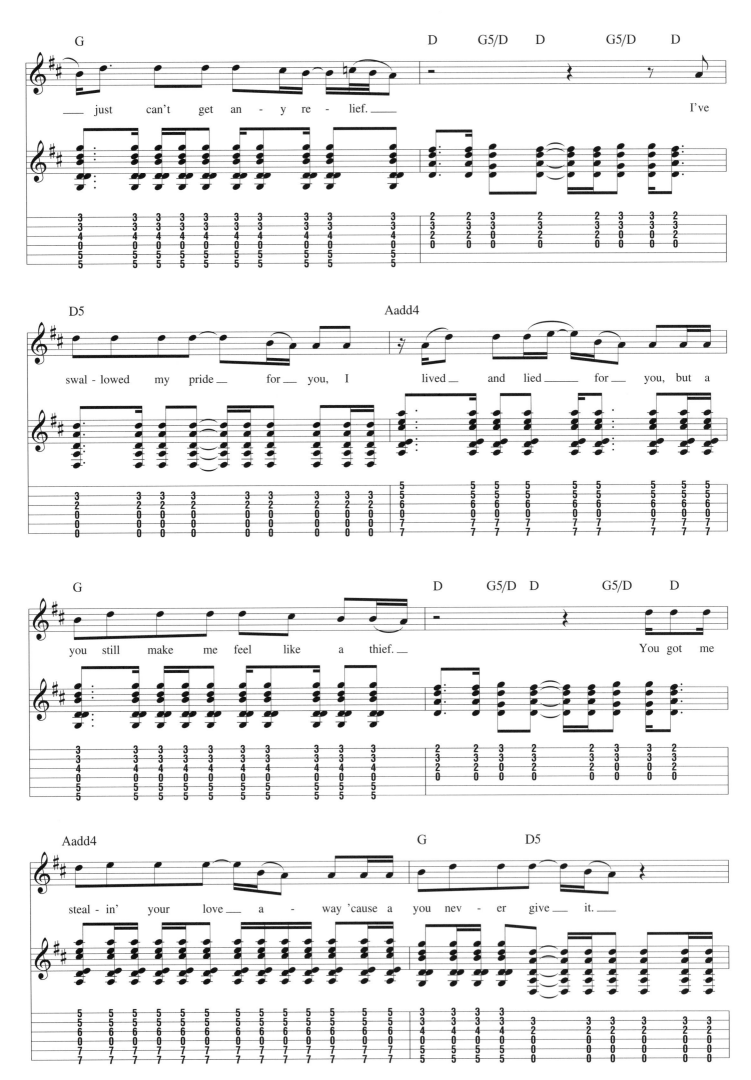

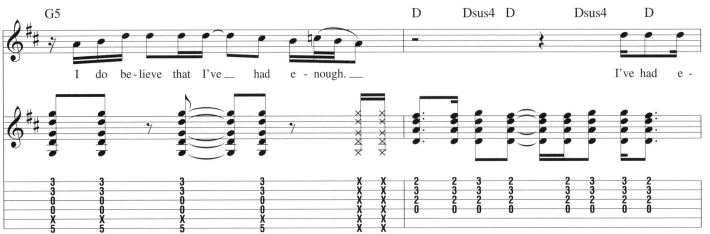

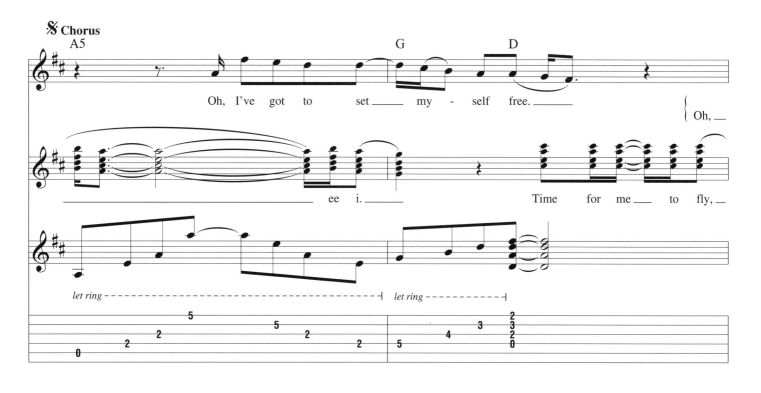

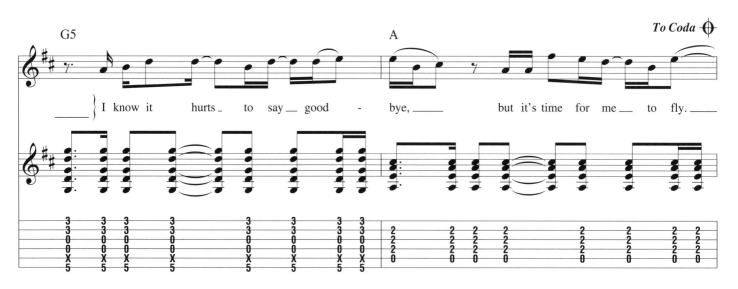

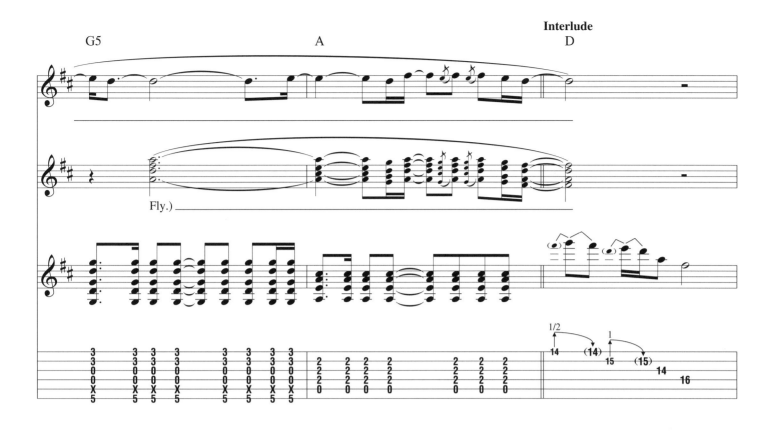

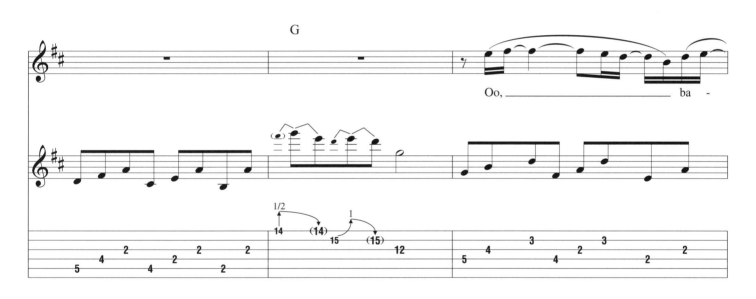

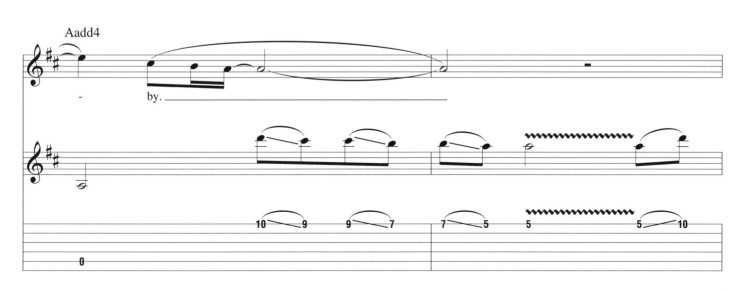

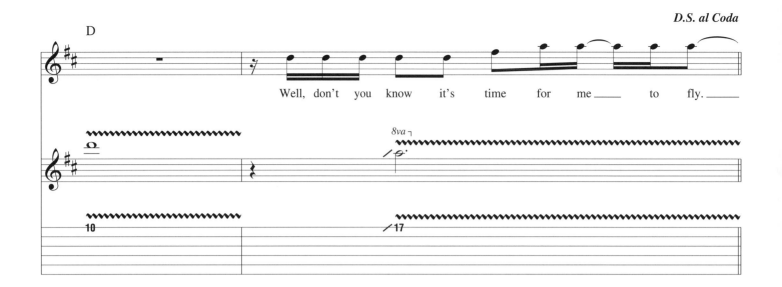

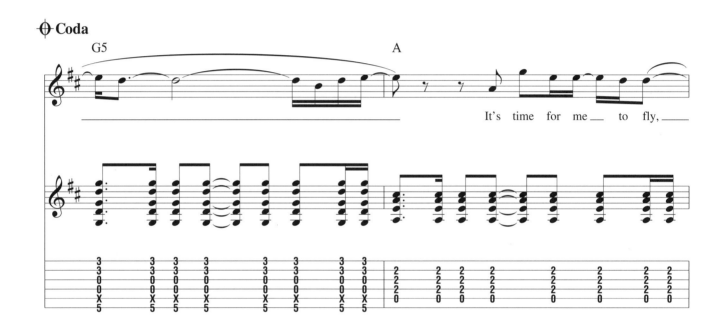

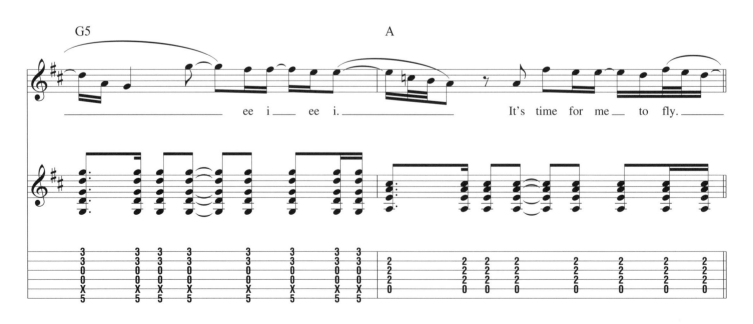

104

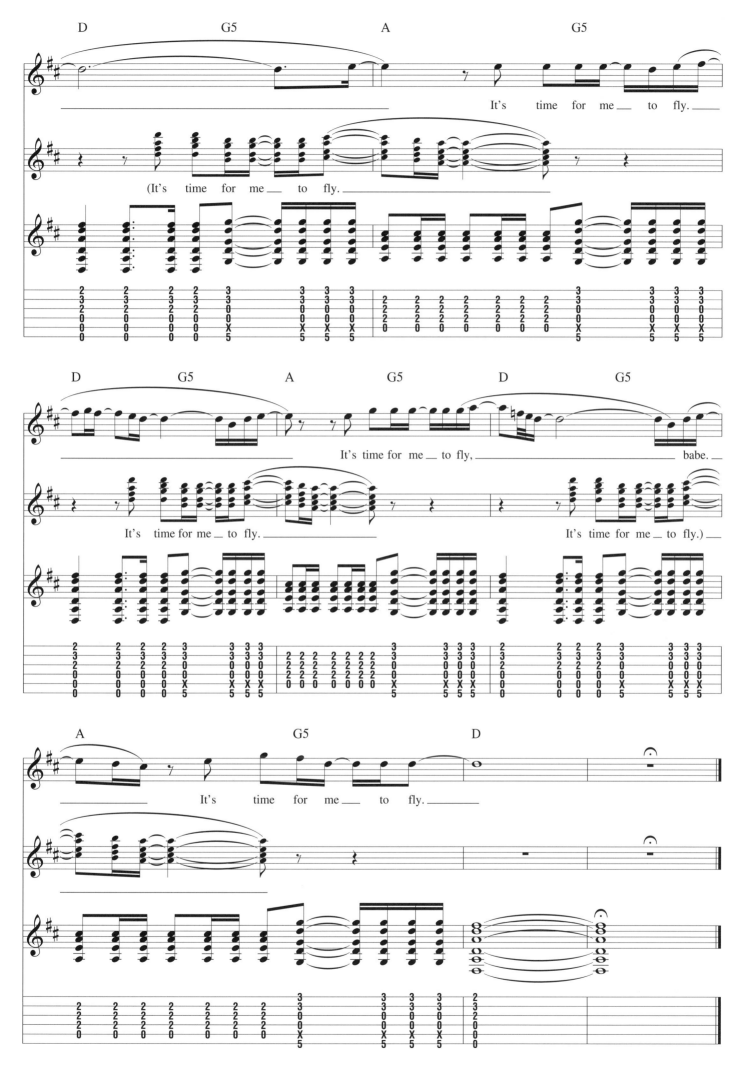

Walk on the Wild Side

Words and Music by Lou Reed

Tune down 1 whole step:
(low to high) D-G-C-F-A-D

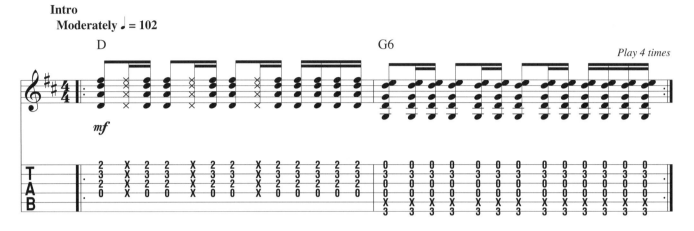

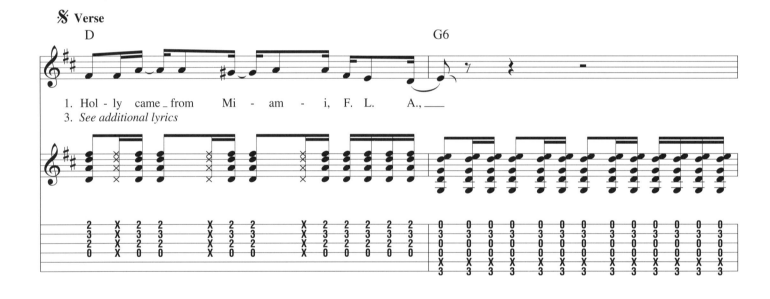

1. Hol - ly came __ from Mi - am - i, F. L. A., __
3. *See additional lyrics*

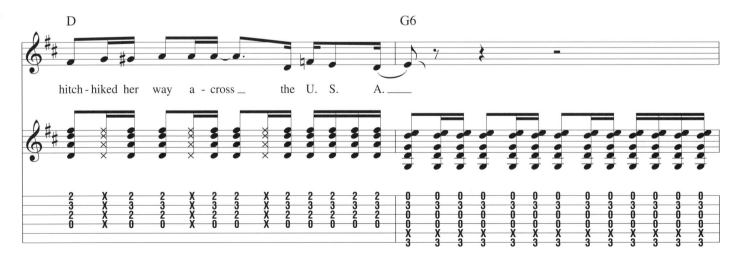

hitch - hiked her way a - cross __ the U. S. A. __

Copyright © 1972 Oakfield Avenue Music Ltd.
Copyright Renewed
All Rights Administered by Spirit One Music
International Copyright Secured   All Rights Reserved

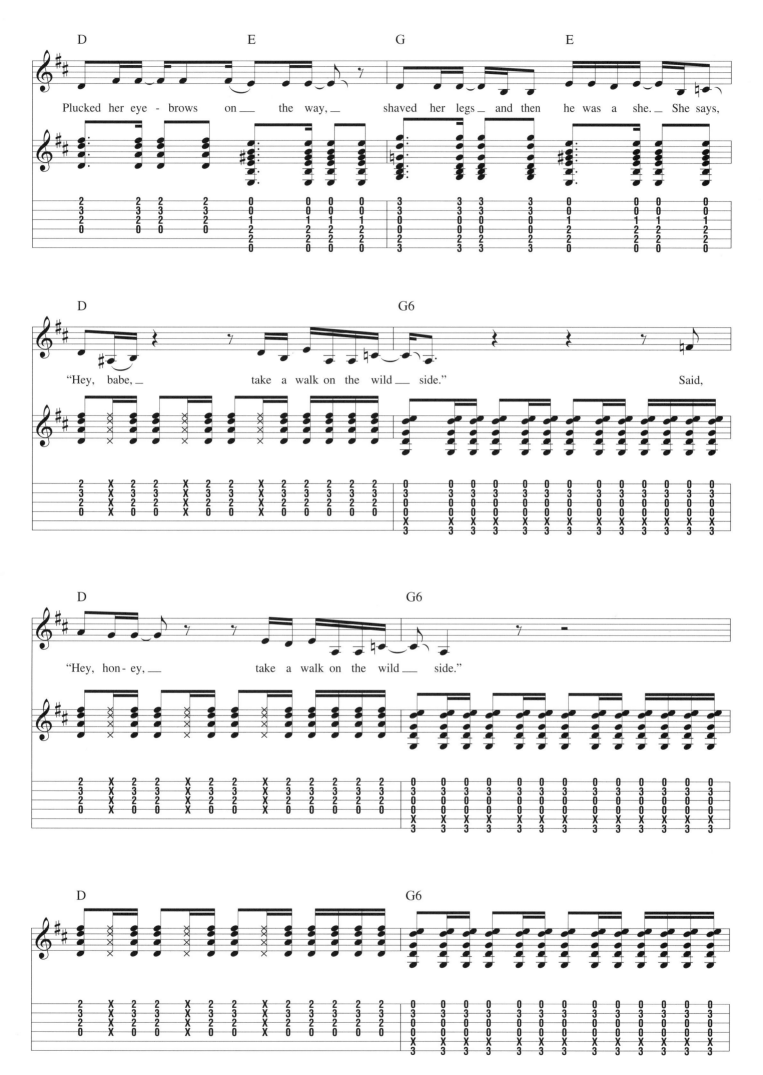

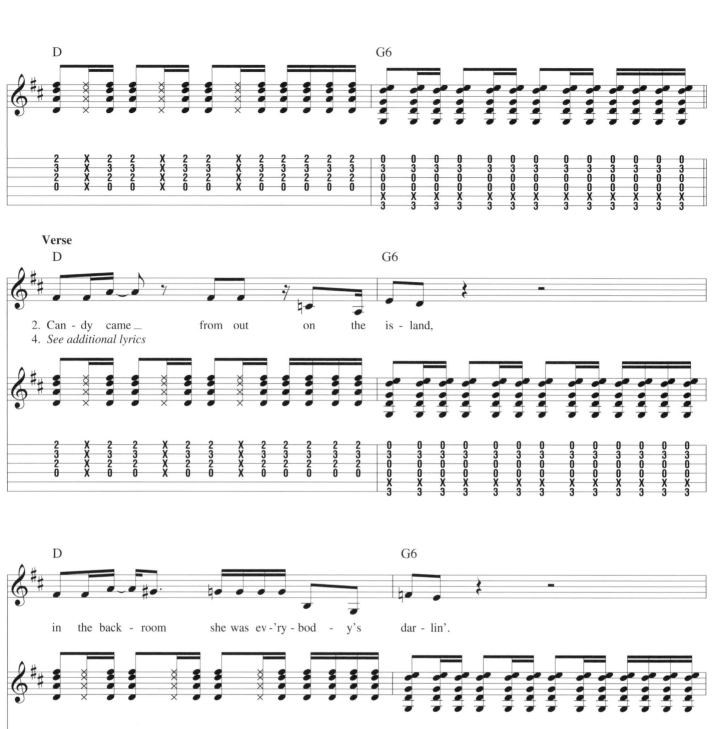

Verse

2. Can - dy came _ from out on the is - land,
4. *See additional lyrics*

in the back - room she was ev - 'ry - bod - y's dar - lin'.

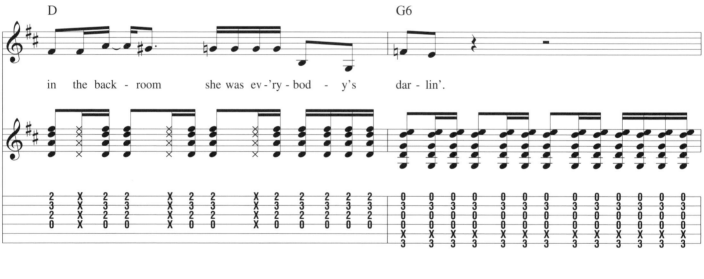

But she nev - er lost _ her head, _ e - ven when _ she was giv - in' head. _ She says,

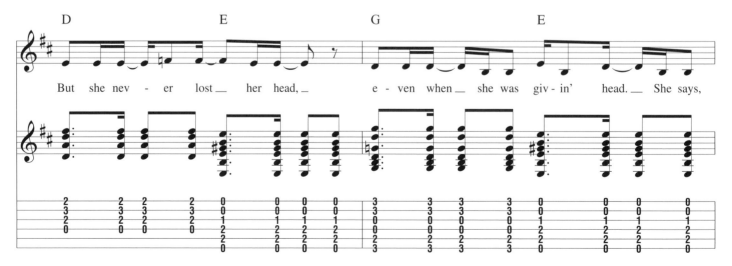

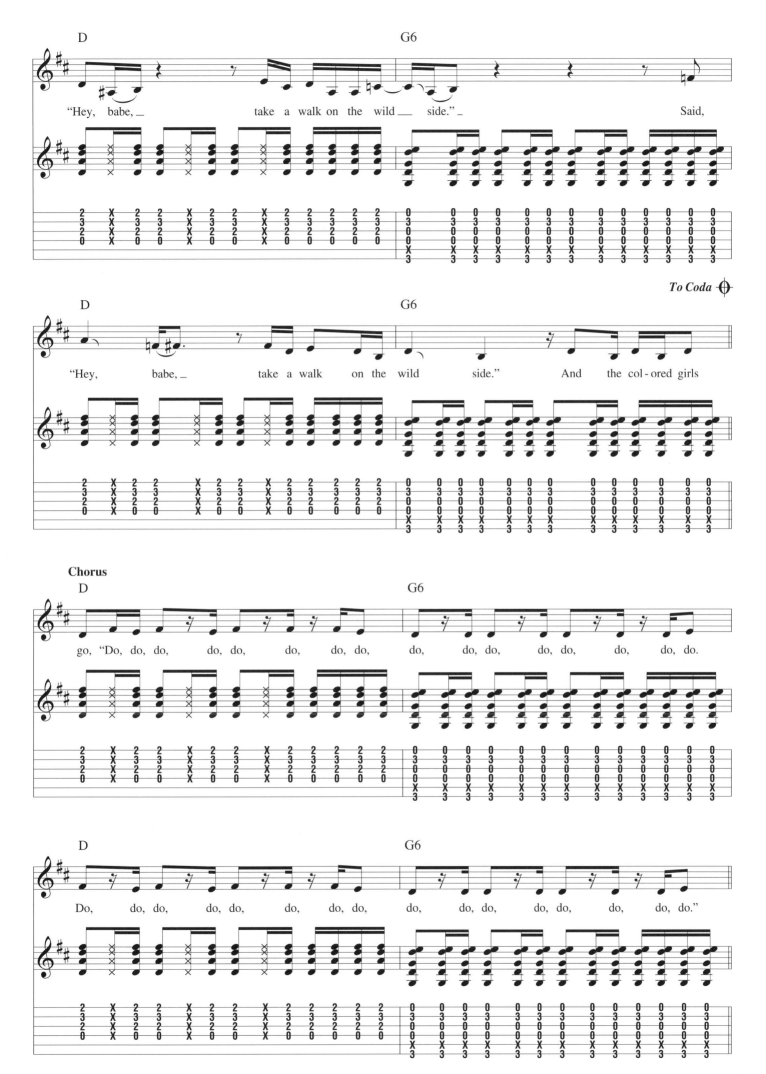

(Do,   do, do,   do, do,   do,   do, do,   do,   do, do,   do, do,   do,   do, do.

Do.) _____

D.S. al Coda

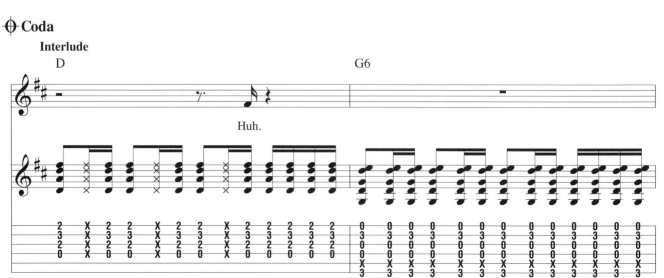

Coda

Interlude

Huh.

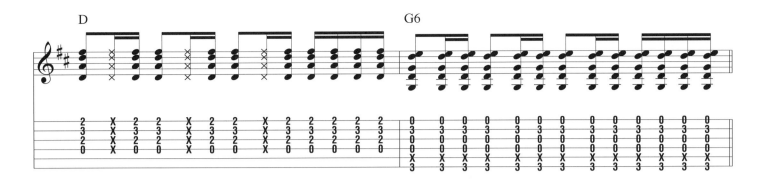

Verse

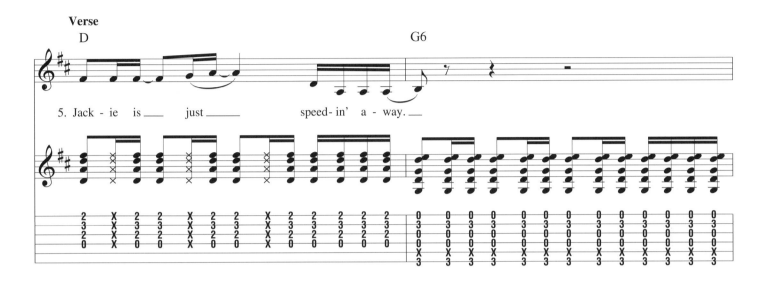

5. Jack- ie is ___ just ___ speed- in' a - way. ___

Thought she was ___ James Dean for a day. ___

Then I guess ___ she had ___ to crash. ___ Val - i - um ___ would -'ve helped that bash. She said,

Outro-Sax Solo

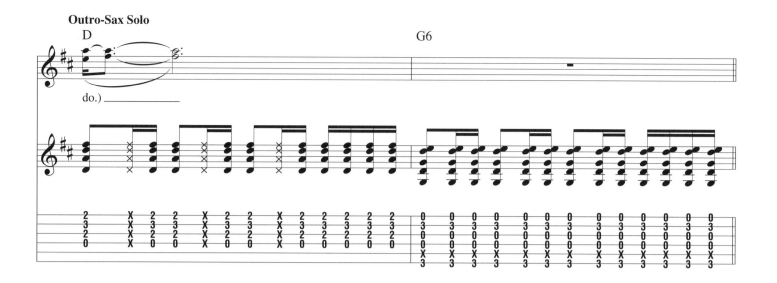

(do.)

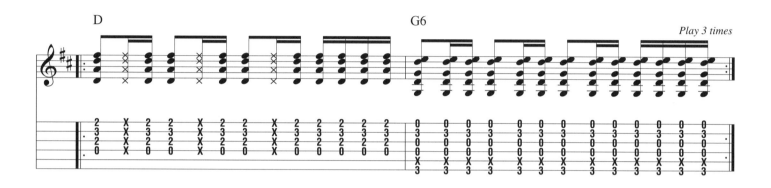

Play 3 times

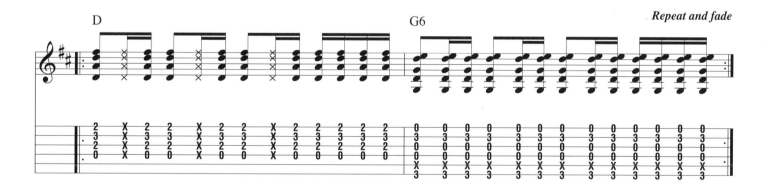

Repeat and fade

Additional Lyrics

3. Little Joe never once gave it away,
   Everybody had to pay and pay.
   A hustle here and a hustle there,
   New York City is the place where they said,
   "Hey, babe, take a walk on the wild side."
   I said, "Hey, Joe, take a walk on the wild side."

4. Sugar plum fairy came and hit the streets,
   Looking for soul food and a place to eat.
   Went to the Apollo; you should have seen them go, go, go.
   They said, "Hey, sugar, take a walk on the wild side."
   I said, "Hey, babe, take a walk on the wild side."
   Alright. Huh.

Working Class Hero

Words and Music by John Lennon

Copyright © 1970 Yoko Ono, Sean Lennon and Julian Lennon
Copyright Renewed
All Rights Administered by Sony/ATV Music Publishing LLC, 8 Music Square West, Nashville, TN 37203
International Copyright Secured   All Rights Reserved

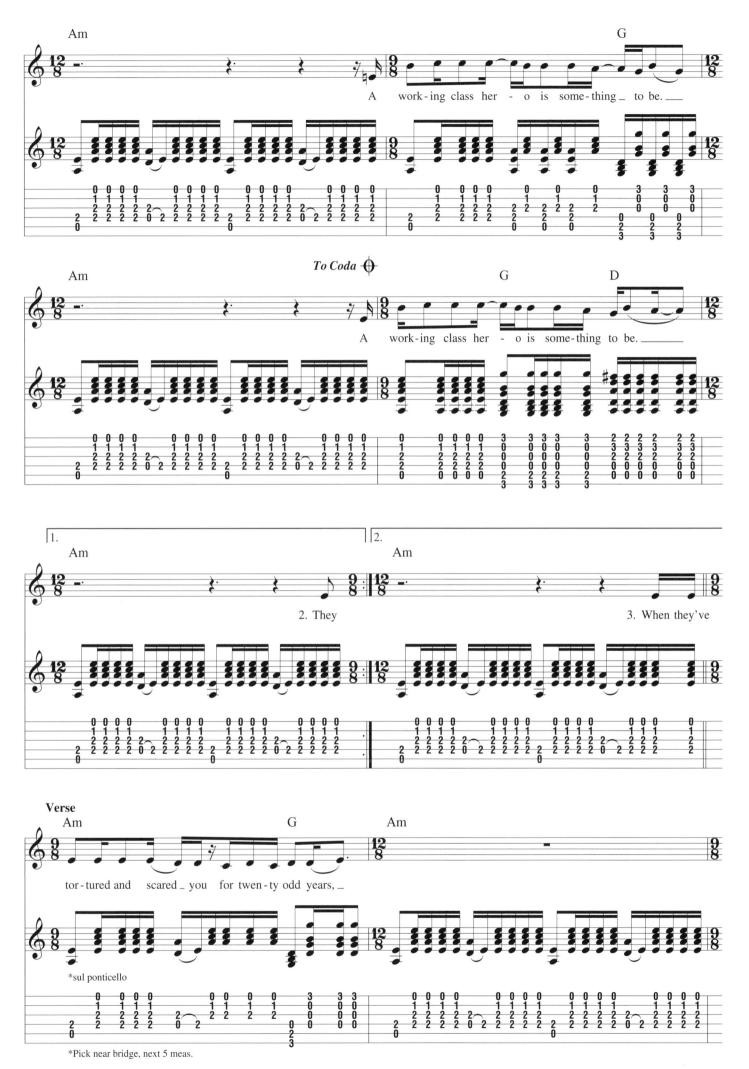

A work-ing class her - o is some-thing to be.

To Coda

A work-ing class her - o is some-thing to be.

1.

2.

2. They

3. When they've

Verse

tor-tured and scared you for twen-ty odd years,

*sul ponticello

*Pick near bridge, next 5 meas.

then they ex - pect you to pick a ca - reer. ___ When you

can't re - al - ly func - tion you're so full of fear. ___ A

work - ing class he - ro is some - thing to be. ___ A

D.S. al Coda

work - ing class he - ro is some - thing to be. ___ 4. Keep you

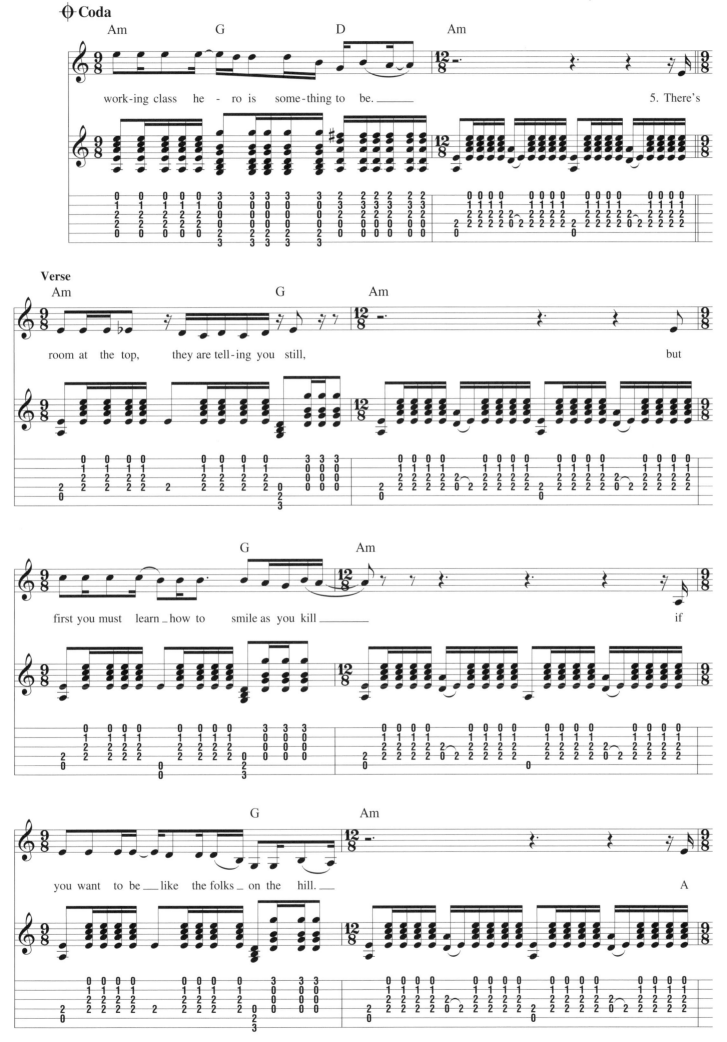

working class hero is something to be. _____ 5. There's

Verse

room at the top, they are telling you still, but

first you must learn _ how to smile as you kill _____ if

you want to be _ like the folks _ on the hill. _ A

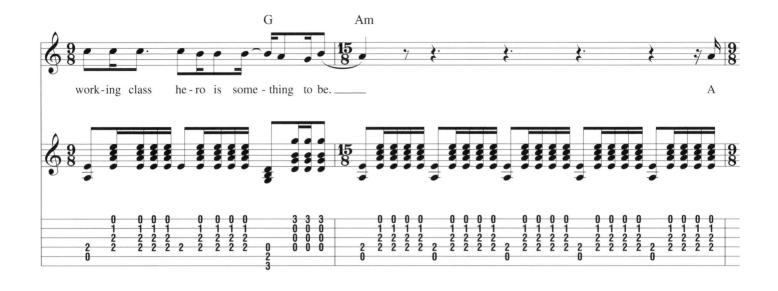

working class hero is something to be. _____ A

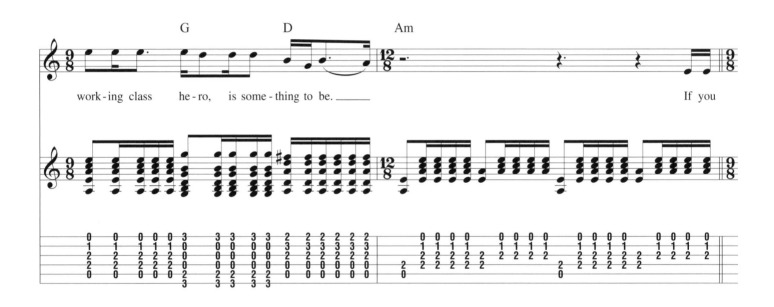

working class hero, is something to be. _____ If you

Outro

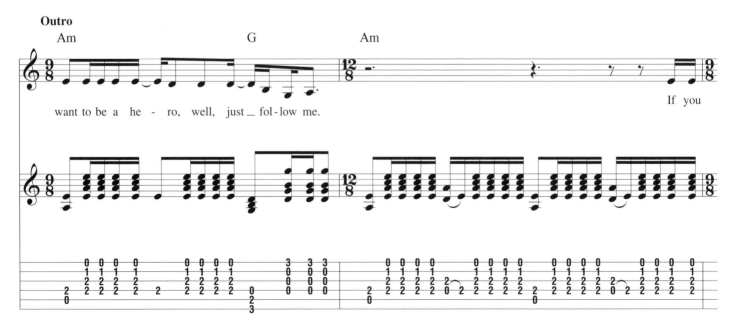

want to be a hero, well, just _ fol-low me. If you

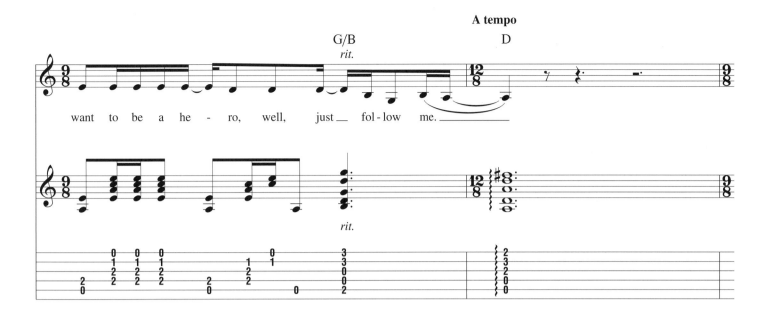

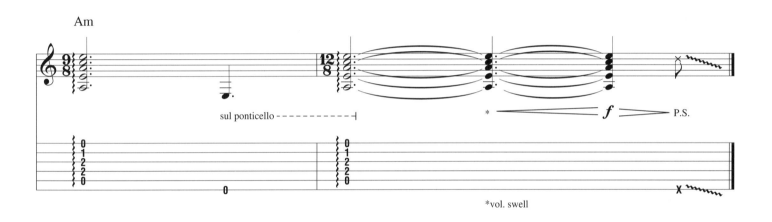

*vol. swell

Additional Lyrics

2. They hurt you at home and they hit you at school.
   They hate you if you're clever and they despise a fool,
   'Till you're so fucking crazy you can't follow their rules.

3. When they've tortured and scared you for twenty odd years
   Then they expect you to pick a career,
   When you can't really function you're so full of fear.

4. Keep you doped with religion and sex and T.V.
   And you think you're so clever and classless and free.
   But you're still fucking peasants as far as I can see.

Guitar Notation Legend

THE MUSICAL STAFF shows pitches and rhythms and is divided by bar lines into measures. Pitches are named after the first seven letters of the alphabet.

TABLATURE graphically represents the guitar fingerboard. Each horizontal line represents a string, and each number represents a fret.

Notes:

Strings:

4th string, 2nd fret

1st & 2nd strings open, played together

open D chord

HALF-STEP BEND: Strike the note and bend up 1/2 step.

WHOLE-STEP BEND: Strike the note and bend up one step.

GRACE NOTE BEND: Strike the note and bend up as indicated. The first note does not take up any time.

SLIGHT (MICROTONE) BEND: Strike the note and bend up 1/4 step.

BEND AND RELEASE: Strike the note and bend up as indicated, then release back to the original note. Only the first note is struck.

PRE-BEND: Bend the note as indicated, then strike it.

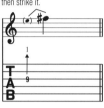

VIBRATO: The string is vibrated by rapidly bending and releasing the note with the fretting hand.

PALM MUTING: The note is partially muted by the pick hand lightly touching the string(s) just before the bridge.

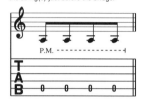

HAMMER-ON: Strike the first (lower) note with one finger, then sound the higher note (on the same string) with another finger by fretting it without picking.

PULL-OFF: Place both fingers on the notes to be sounded. Strike the first note and without picking, pull the finger off to sound the second (lower) note.

LEGATO SLIDE: Strike the first note and then slide the same fret-hand finger up or down to the second note. The second note is not struck.

SHIFT SLIDE: Same as legato slide, except the second note is struck.

TRILL: Very rapidly alternate between the notes indicated by continuously hammering on and pulling off.

TAPPING: Hammer ("tap") the fret indicated with the pick-hand index or middle finger and pull off to the note fretted by the fret hand.

NATURAL HARMONIC: Strike the note while the fret-hand lightly touches the string directly over the fret indicated.

PINCH HARMONIC: The note is fretted normally and a harmonic is produced by adding the edge of the thumb or the tip of the index finger of the pick hand to the normal pick attack.

TREMOLO PICKING: The note is picked as rapidly and continuously as possible.

VIBRATO BAR DIVE AND RETURN: The pitch of the note or chord is dropped a specified number of steps (in rhythm) then returned to the original pitch.

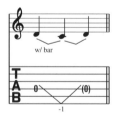

VIBRATO BAR SCOOP: Depress the bar just before striking the note, then quickly release the bar.

VIBRATO BAR DIP: Strike the note and then immediately drop a specified number of steps, then release back to the original pitch.

Additional Musical Definitions

(accent) · Accentuate note (play it louder)

(staccato) · Play the note short

D.S. al Coda · Go back to the sign (𝄉), then play until the measure marked "*To Coda*," then skip to the section labelled "*Coda*."

D.C. al Fine · Go back to the beginning of the song and play until the measure marked "*Fine*" (end).

Fill · Label used to identify a brief melodic figure which is to be inserted into the arrangement.

N.C. · No Chord

 · Repeat measures between signs.

· When a repeated section has different endings, play the first ending only the first time and the second ending only the second time.